SPIRAL STAIRCASE PROJECT MANAGEMENT

SPIRAL STAIRCASE PROJECT MANAGEMENT

A FRAMEWORK TO SUCCEED COMPLEX-COGNITIVE PROJECTS

JOHN ROBERT

Notion Press

Old No. 38, New No. 6
McNichols Road, Chetpet
Chennai - 600 031

First Published by Notion Press 2017
Copyright © John Robert 2017
All Rights Reserved.

ISBN
Hardcase: 978-1-946714-16-9
Paperback: 978-1-946641-68-7

This book has been published with all efforts taken to make the material error-free after the consent of the author. However, the author and the publisher do not assume and hereby disclaim any liability to any party for any loss, damage, or disruption caused by errors or omissions, whether such errors or omissions result from negligence, accident, or any other cause.

No part of this book may be used, reproduced in any manner whatsoever without written permission from the author, except in the case of brief quotations embodied in critical articles and reviews.

Dedicated to my 'network,' which consists of leaders, project team members and fellow project managers, who questioned the traditional practices of project management—and which sowed the seed for this book

Table of Contents

Preface ix

Introduction 1

Genesis of project management and takeaways for today's scenario ... 3

Part 1: Insider's view of project management 13

The Scheduling Challenge: Astrologer or planner 17

The Execution Challenge: Clock vs. Compass 26

The Execution Challenge: Effort and Effect 28

The Gap: Estimate, Commitment and Delivery 30

Part 2: The changing paradigm of project management 33

The Ultimate Shift: From triple constraints to the purpose 37

Paradigm shift of projects from Industrial Age to Knowledge Era .. 40

Transforming triple constraints to triple opportunities 46

Part 3: A new framework for today's cognitive projects 59

Staircase and Project Management 61

Challenges in Managing Projects 66

Spiral Staircase Explained 70

Foundation Principles 73

Principle 1: Purpose of the project is the foremost important goal of a project 73

Principle 2: Progressively elaborated projects are progressively planned 74

Principle 3: Assumptions can go wrong 75

Principle 4: Effort and effect are not directly proportional 76

Principle 5: Culture of engagement is a key enabler in cognitive projects 77

Principle 6: Projects get influenced by the external environment 78

Principle 7: Projects are like a relay race, not a marathon 79

SSPM framework 83

True north of projects and SSPM Framework 85

Five core processes of SSPM Framework 88

Core Process 1: Project Initiation: Define the POPE 88

Core Process 2: Initial Planning: Create a Project Master Plan 96

    The Architecture of SSPM 103

Core Process 3: Project Execution—Focus, Plan, Process and Move on Watertight schedules 106

Core Process 4: Project Controls in SSPM: Platform reviews 118

Core Process 5: Project Closeout: Deliver and seek feedback 126

Part 4: Program Management: SSPM for Multi-projects 133

Profile of Project Leaders in SSPM 151

Fostering Change and WIFM 154

About the Author 165

Glossary of Terms 167

Bibliography 169

List of Illustrations 171

Preface

Hundreds of laborers were engaged in various activities on a project site. Enthused by the massive construction activities taking place there, a passerby approached and asked the first laborer whom he encountered, "What are you doing?" The man replied, "I work here and my job is to remove dirt from the earth." The passerby walked further and asked yet another laborer the same question. That man replied, "Can't you see what am I doing? I am preparing the plaster. This is an essential material for this construction." The laborer moved on.

The passerby spotted another busy worker and asked him, "Gentleman, what are you doing?" The worker replied with a proud smile, "We are building a temple—this is going to be a place of worship. Many men and women are going to come here to find peace and experience God."

A resource who is connected to the core purpose of the project can make a big difference. Wouldn't it be great if our project teams were made up of inspired, involved resources? It is unusual to start a project management book with an Eastern parable—however, this book puts forth the approach needed to deliver projects successfully, even if it may be unusual. The inspired construction worker's ownership in the project may not seem relevant to project management techniques that we use today—which are more focused on metrics and efficiency. However, the time has come for us to re-examine current and traditional practices, and to see if they are still relevant in today's world, where human intelligence makes a big difference. It would be risky to assume that the body of knowledge can be 'unboxed' and put into practice for every project, right away. Also, while most current practices are valid and applicable for many projects, a different approach is required to engage a worker when it comes to cognitive projects.

This book examines the practices that are being followed blindly, raises questions and kindles thoughts on a new approach by which projects could be carried out. It is meant for those who seek an alternate way to engage their workforce and aim for passionate execution rather than being stifled by an analytical framework. It is written for:

- Today's leaders in project, program and portfolio management, who are striving to deliver results through cognitive projects
- Tomorrow's leaders, who are witnessing evolution of management and leadership in knowledge and conceptual era
- Organizations that are dependent on cognitive projects and rely on human capital rather than machines
- Scholars who seek an alternative methodology in project management
- Research organizations

- Fellow project management practitioners and academicians who aim to re-examine the current models
- Professionals in startups, research and development (R&D) and business ventures who need a structured yet flexible, agile and nimble approach to accomplish their endeavors
- Anyone who is looking for a fresh perspective towards managing projects

The structure of this book

This book has four parts.

Part 1: Insider's view of project management

This section details the practical aspect of projects, and some of the challenges in initiating, planning, organizing, executing, controlling and closing a project. It looks at why projects are failing, and how traditional practices unsuccessfully attempt to determine and deliver the analytical framework of the projects. This section draws on my own experience, and that of my mentors and fellow project managers. A significant section is derived from unconventional thinkers of our age, who consistently pressure-test the traditional practices in managing projects.

Part 2: Changing paradigm of projects

The need for a new framework is evidenced by the shift in the nature of projects over the ages. Today's projects are more cognitive and less dependent on machines, unlike two decades ago. Today, machines only complement the intellectual process and do not determine the success of the projects. There is a need to engage the heads, hearts and hands of the people who create the products and services. Applying rules meant for machines undervalues the power of creative, intellectual capabilties of these people.

Part 3: A new framework for today's cognitive projects

The need for a new framework, explained in part 2, and hence part 3, deals with the foundation principles and the framework for cognitive projects. A fresh progressive model is proposed and evaluated in place of deterministic project management methodology, with a target to turn around the triple constraints.

Part 4: Program management

Part 4 deals with the application of a new set of rules in multi-project environments. The new approach is proven to be applicable for program and portfolio context. While facing a resource crunch, the difference between 'early kill' and 'late kill' of projects makes a lot of difference from the resource perspective. This part examines the application of the new framework in such an environment to create superior results.

What should you expect?

I believe this book will bring in...

- Examination of practices that are being adapted to all projects without question
- Better understanding about the changing paradigm of projects
- A courageous approach to aligning projects with their core purpose
- A sense of urgency towards adopting new ways of working
- A practical approach to handling cognitive projects effectively, to bring out the best in these projects and not to limit it to the time cost and scope framework
- A structured approach of consistent processes to enable effective execution, and to design an analytical framework in line with the DNA of the project

It is important to recognize that I have not assumed any obligation towards aligning with the 'commonly accepted practices' of project management, but have tried to keep myself open to the ways in which we could create better project management ecosystems. Also, the purpose is not to load the reader with overwhelming data that may not be usable in a practical context. The purpose is to make a paradigm shift in the execution of projects based on real-life experience. This is an effort to apply practical experience while re-examining project management practices, and to arrive at a simpler, more meaningful framework that is in line with the nature of the projects of the day. A project is efficient when it meets its time, cost and analytical framework but it can be successful only when it fulfills the purpose. The framework illustrated in this book is an attempt to make project efficient and successful. In perusing this goal, I welcome you, the readers, to approach this book with an open mind, and to explore if there is a better way in carrying out our projects. Indeed, I am not stating that this book is the complete cure for all problems in managing projects but that the reader will see a metaphor that vividly explains the DNA of projects and gain a fresh perspective. This will also lead you towards an uncomplicated, practical, workable framework that consists of mutually reinforcing practices that enable far superior results from your cognitive projects. This is my promise.

Introduction

The power of a concept lies in its simplicity. All that is required for one to understand this book's primary concept is to walk through a spiral staircase. Every management discipline had evolved through the infusion of new skills, tools and mindset. While there are advanced tools available today, the project management predominantly relies on the concepts developed in the nineteenth century for the military and for the moon mission. These techniques were adequate back then, and may be still relevant for many industrial age projects. However, the Information Age has its own set of challenges and complexities to deal with, and requires a new set of rules. Here not only machines but also knowledge and skill of the project team determine the success of the project. Hence, the time has come to move from a project-centric to a customer-centric way of working, from rigid rules to a flexible framework. Research has shown that a dedicated workforce is not adequate, but volunteerism is required to make a significant difference to improving performance. Is it possible to cultivate volunteerism by having command and control based management methods? This is a call for a new mindset, a vision for making a difference through project management.

As many of the other management practices have evolved a lot in recent times to adapt to the information era, this is my humble effort to sow a seed in the ocean of project management for a different thinking. This is an invitation for the project management community to think beyond the triple constraint.

When things are not going the way as planned in projects, I wonder about what happened to the project management frameworks and time-tested principles. Why is there a sense of uncertainty when it comes to completing projects on time, in scope and within cost? At the outset, it would seem that an optimistic estimate, improper planning or under-performance are the causes of project failure. However, real-world experience teaches us that failure is due by the very nature of the project. Several new aspects unfold during the execution of a project, which are not known at the time of initial planning. I have also evidenced that the planning team spends more time and energy in accounting for these unknown aspects in the estimate. As a result, they come up with granular schedule estimates. However, granular planning defeats the purpose and results in inaccurate estimates. Companies seldom finish projects within the stipulated time, cost and scope, when an unanticipated, additional work has to be done, which demands much more resources and time than that anticipated in the 'project scope document.' Hence, the answer lies not in the tools that are being used but in the very soul of projects. The purpose or the value to be created by the project needs to be put forth before everything else—even before time, cost and scope. The compass should be used to drive the project rather than the clock. Rather than trying to force-fit a project into an available framework, this is an effort to explore an appropriate project management framework that fits the purpose of the project.

Genesis of project management and takeaways for today's scenario

Around the world, companies have undertaken projects in all fields—from building mega structures to developing software to inventing life-saving medicines. The project is a creative process and that has been in practice from ever since human started creating shelters for their safe habitat. The first very project in accordance with various beliefs is the creation of the world and mankind. Even that 'first project' had a systematic and method-driven approach in the creative process, according to the greatest story ever told. This creative process, as per the *Bible*, is a primary inspiration for this framework. However, unlike other management disciplines, project management was not recognized as a distinct management discipline until the last century. Significant development began in the 1910s with the Gantt chart, developed by Henry Gantt and in the 1950s, with the invention of the Critical Path Method (CPM) by the DuPont Corporation, as well as the Program Evaluation Review Technique (PERT) by the United States of America's Navy's Polaris Project. These triggered significant development of project management as a discipline on its own merit, and, since then, PERT—in conjunction with CPM—has been adapted for managing projects.

Today, there are different schools of thoughts and methodologies, such as PRINCE2®, PMBOK® standard, Agile® and CCPM that have been put in place for project management. Particularly over the last two decades, project management has progressed as a discipline with intensive efforts in education, and industries have started to recognize and apply project management standards, tools, and techniques to drive their projects efficiently. Since the evolution of project management as a discipline, several changes have taken place in the industry—each change is an opportunity to evaluate the current state and to recalibrate it for better results.

Seven factors have restructured the way in which projects are being executed:

1. **Projects are becoming increasingly complex:** The element of unpredictability is growing by the day. Many of the tasks undertaken in projects are of an iterative nature. Unlike in the past, where one had a fixed scope definition, today's projects call for greater responsiveness and flexibility.

2. **Projects are no longer executed in adiabatic conditions:** Projects no longer operate in an insulated environment, and seldom does a project progress without the influence of external factors. The project's viability changes during execution, and the assumptions made about its feasibility

are consistently challenged by factors such as rapid technology obsolesce, shift in the customer preferences, shorter product life cycle, new inventions and competing products in the marketplace. Often, this might challenge the sustained viability of the products, services or results that a project aims to deliver—and these factors might even hasten the termination of a project. Hence, there is a greater need for responsiveness to external factors.

3. **There is a shift in dependence:** Today, projects rely more on the human intellect, while most of the projects in the last century were primarily dependent on machines. The efficiency-focused methodology was well suited for those projects, but does not guarantee a positive outcome for cognition-based projects that are driven by a knowledge workforce. The analytical framework for measuring the success or failures of projects also, unfortunately, disregards the inherent uncertainty and often accounts only for variability. This tends to stifle the creative process of projects, and even acts as an impediment to unleashing the true potential of the creative process.

4. **Projects are extensive and challenging to manage:** The width and depth of projects are much greater, and projects spanning more than a couple of years are being undertaken. An extraordinary level of complexities needs to be dealt with in order to deliver projects successfully. Also, many aspects

unfold as a project progresses. Hence, sticking to the pre-determined estimates, made during the initiation, are less feasible.

5. **Maintaining pace amid constant change:** Projects need to be agile and nimble, as the ecosystem at the time of completion of the project could be very different from the time it was initiated. The speed at which decisions are taken determines the success of a project—and a greater number of course corrections are needed during execution than what was necessary a decade back. The project team needs to be more agile and nimble in order to make adjustments to the project so as to sustain its viability when the product or services are delivered into the market. Requirements do not remain stable and swift response to the developments acts as a differentiating factor for winning with projects.

6. **Evolution of types of projects:** Projects have transformed considerably from the military and industrial ages to the Information Age—from brick-and-mortar to radical innovation. The ratio of brick and motor projects to cognitive projects suggests that it is skewed towards the later type. This includes the innovation drive, startups, and research and development projects to name few. Projects in today's world require new skill sets, tool sets and mindsets—hence, businesses have redefined the operating rules. Along with the general management and leadership methodologies, projects also have to

adapt to a new set of standards to continue to be relevant, and to contribute to today's marketplace.

7. **Evolution of the intellectual workforce:** Today's project team members are more passionate about their profession and are considered as 'partners' in the business. There is a shift in the culture of the workforce. Dedicated, skilled, trained labor is a thing of past—organizations now look for out-of-the-box thinking and creativity. Intrapreneurs with complete ownership are needed to deliver the complex projects of today. Unleashing the maximum potential of human resources is the need of the hour. An enabling environment, motivation and sense of belonging are required in today's ecosystem. A volunteer workforce enables greater productivity, when compared to the controlled laborers with carrot-and-stick methods of motivation.

Today's projects are more complex to plan, difficult to execute, vulnerable for delays and much harder to recover. Given this, there are several other factors that reinforce the need for a new approach in which projects are being managed.

A typical project lifecycle consists of initiation, planning, organizing, execution and control and closeout. A project is initiated to deliver an intended purpose, and detailed planning is done upfront, after which the necessary resources and investment are lined up. Then, the project is executed, and controls are put in place to ensure that it is progressing in line with the set plan. Upon completion, the closeout procedure is carried out. As such, there are four core processes:

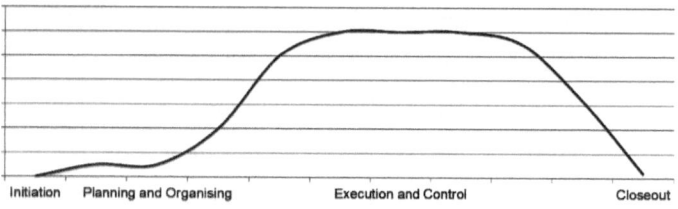

Fig 1. Traditional deterministic model project lifecycle and efforts in every phase of the project

Initiation: In this process, objectives and cost-benefit calculations are established. If the project is found to be viable, it is approved. The sponsor plays a vital role here, as he/she is the one who funds the project and is often the internal or external customers as well. Identification of project stakeholders and development of project charter are some of the aspects dealt with in this process.

Planning and organizing: The success or failure of a project is determined by the planning process—hence, it is considered as a vital process in project management—some businesses are more focused on this aspect more than any other project management processes. The planning process covers aspects such as scope, time, cost, quality and resources involved and required to deliver the project. There are many planning methods, such as network analysis, critical path methods, critical chain methodology, spiral method and agile methods. Each of these techniques aims to quantify uncertainty and provide a clear path to the project team to execute the projects on time, within the scope and budgeted cost. Planning is not merely developing a project schedule but it involves all the things that are required for a project. While the baseline has been set by a rigorous planning process, organizing takes care of lining up all the resources, capital, equipment, procedures and knowledge required for executing the project.

Execution and control: The implementation team takes up the project, utilizes the budget given and performs the activities in order to produce the results. By and large, the execution team is given the mandate of achieving the pre-determined goals that were laid out in the planning process. Any deviation has to go through a scope change process. The project controls play a vital role in tracking, reviewing and regulating the project in order to deliver it within the pre-determined time, cost and scope, and are helpful in maintaining discipline on the shop floor.

Closeout: The closeout process consists of the processes performed to finalize all activities across the project to formally conclude a project. This includes comparing results with the objectives laid out at the time of initiation. This is an essential but often ignored process in many projects. Project closeout plays a vital role in terms of providing maintenance and upkeeping of the product or services in the interest of ensuring the continued success of the product's life cycle.

Many companies log the lessons learned, and encourage teams to learn from the mistakes.

In many ways, current project management methodologies advocate for planning once, and delivering from then onwards for the entire life cycle of the project. When both planning and organizing are done upfront, it is often referred as a 'deterministic model.' The estimation of cost, time and resources is also done upfront, based on the initial assessment. These estimates would imply that there is no room for changes over the course of the project. If a project consumes more time and resources than the pre-determined parameters, it has to undergo scope change or deviation approval to secure additional funds and resources. Quite often, projects that deviate from the initial estimates are termed 'failed projects.' This approach may not be compatible with today's world, where the complexity of projects is ever increasing, duration of projects is longer, and there is a greater need for flexibility. So, let us look at some of the parameters that call for a new way of thinking in carrying out projects.

Integration fiasco: Projects are usually managed as if they were a single, long endeavor from start to finish—in reality, a large project consists of several sections that are co-created by multi-disciplinary expert groups, each of whom has its own pace, rules of engagement and complexity. Assuming all of them to be similar, and applying a generic rule to all would undermine the creative capability and intricacies of the different groups. Moreover, integration of the entire project as a single endeavor results in multiplying the amount of communication needed in the name of keeping the upstream and downstream stakeholders. One of the issues faced by today's executives is the need to deal with the problem of plenty when it comes to e-mails. They need to spend a significant amount of their time in reading and responding to hundreds of e-mails. The superfluous communication, which results from the integration of the entire project, dilutes the focus of individual work streams and saps the productivity of resources. Projects are not like marathons—they are better compared to relay races that consist of interdependent sections that need to be carried out by several different work streams. Treating all of them similarly and planning for all of them in the same way may not be an efficient way of getting the maximum benefit from each of them. Each of these segments needs flexibility and autonomy for the sake of carrying out the project successfully.

Projects are driven by analytical frameworks: The success or failure of today's projects is determined by their ability to meet the analytical framework. If a project is able to meet the pre-determined cost, scope and time, it is considered a success. Deviation in the timeline is termed as failure, and disregards all the work done by the project team thus far. The evolution of project management as a discipline is centered on making sure that the project delivers the product on time and within the given budget and scope. These three yardsticks are used quite often in the analytical framework of measuring a project. In reality, there are several internal factors ('inside-out') and market development factors ('outside-in') that determine the success or failure of a project. Currently, these events do not seem to be accounted for except during a scope change. This has nothing to do with the teachings of prevailing project management frameworks, which reinstate the need for re-planning projects in several intervals due to progressive elaboration. However, in reality, these frameworks are highly misunderstood and are applied merely as deterministic calculations. The more deterministic the estimation, the more vulnerable the project is. Even by a simple mathematical model, the probable estimate of tasks does not result in a high probability of completing a project within its target—hence, the traditional project management practices put forth several impediments for seamless execution of a project and does not measure up to the needs of today's projects.

Completing a project on time, within the scope and cost estimate are considered top priorities. However, when uncertainty is a primary challenge, complying with the analytical framework is seldom feasible. The objective of a project is to deliver unique products or services to a customer, as per the definition—but if one dissolves the boundaries of this definition, a project is something that is meant to fulfill a purpose for a customer or a stakeholder. Quite often, the scope of a project ignores the core purpose and focuses on the analytical framework. There is a need to shift the focus from mere numbers, and all the metrics should be intertwined around the purpose of the project.

Part 1

The insider's story of project management

While there are many models in project management that try to predict the date on which the project can be delivered and the budget required, the reality is that almost half the projects are termed 'unsuccessful.' This is in accordance with the analytical framework used for the project success measurement. Statistics published by prominent project management authorities demonstrate that a majority of the projects end up unsuccessful year on year. It is often quite difficult to precisely predict the duration of a project unless it is carried out by machines. For the tasks executed by human resources, the accuracy can be brought into the estimate with suitable buffers, but this could stretch the schedule and become counterproductive. Hence, the base case and best case estimates are worked out and, quite often, some safety margins are added to derive project schedules and determine the completion targets.

While executing a project, the cascading delays get accumulated and passed on to the subsequent stages. This, in turn, snowballs all the delays and provides very little time to the work stream at the end of the project. This, in effect, stifles the later stage deliverables in a project's lifecycle. Often, steps at the end of the project comprise quality checks or performance verification—these are closest to the customer, which verify the product or services fitment for use. With shorter timelines, these steps are often challenged, which might directly affect the customers' experience.

It is a common belief that the more detailed the project schedule, the higher the probability of meeting the deadline. In reality, this is not true. If the tasks are estimated accurately, it will result in predicting a perfect deadline. Let us assume there are two tasks with ninety percent probability, the Probability of Success (POS) for both tasks to be done together is eighty-one percent. Assume there are ten tasks with ninety percent probability. These ten tasks, all together, will reduce the probability of success of the entire project to thirty-five percent; fifty tasks one after another will result in only 0.5 percent POS. The granularity in tasks does not bring about the predictability of the project deadline, but the accuracy of the tasks does. It is true that nothing should go unnoticed while planning for a project and everything needed to accomplish the purpose of the project should be captured in the schedule, but merely having a detailed schedule does not guarantee on-time delivery.

Another common approach is to have aggressive timelines to help deliver the project faster. This might have helped in industrial projects. However, for R&D or innovation projects, it is not time pressure but volunteerism that works. A sense of ownership and accomplishment motivates the team towards superior efforts. Time pressure is certainly not a motivating factor—it is the carrot-and-stick method of motivation of the Industrial Age. This is not necessarily suitable for knowledge workers, and certainly not for complex cognitive projects.

There are three significant challenges in managing a project today and these are detailed in subsequent chapters.

The Scheduling Challenge: Astrologer or Planner?

What is the right choice—to be accurately wrong or approximately right?

Success in projects often does not depend on how one executes the tasks that are known upfront, but on how one responds to the unknown tasks that are not revealed at the beginning of the project. A project plan is like a map—by following it, the team embarks on a journey to deliver the products or services. Ideally, a plan should provide critical navigation points and a step-by-step sequence of activities that the team could follow and successfully perform the intended objectives.

However, the challenge is to come up with an accurate plan while dealing with some unknown aspects during the planning stage. In the project management fraternity, this is commonly referred to as 'progressively elaborated.' Unlike a typical production task, where all the parameters are known and defined at the start, a project task has several uncertainties that are not identified in the early stages. So, it is seldom possible to prepare a plan for a high level of accuracy or to expect the project to be finished within the initial estimate of cost and time. When a project manager prepares a project schedule, he/she tries to predict some of the unknown elements—so, the project plan includes a list of assumptions while kick-starting the project. This is similar to fortune telling. Quite often, the astrologer's prediction could fail or be inaccurate, but the astrologer is not held accountable for the results. However, a project manager is responsible for his/her plans. When the plan does not materialize as foretold, or if there are cost overruns, schedule overruns and scope changes, the project team is held accountable. A project planner becomes an astrologer with accountability. In effect, the project team or project planner himself/herself appears to be unable to deliver the target. Ironically, this is not about 'who' but 'what.' By looking at the proportion of failed projects against successful ones, we are tempted to believe that the system is designed for time overruns and scope changes. For decades, we were taught to use the average of adding optimistic, pessimistic and four times nominal to mitigate the risk of unpredictable schedules. However, practically determining these factors are often difficult for the work done by human minds. Even if one uses it, it is seldom possible to predict the schedule precisely beyond a point wherein all aspects are clear and vivid. Many times, several activities are given ballpark estimates, believing that the predictions will hold good or that the inaccuracy of the forecast for a few activities will be nullified in larger projects.

While planning for a project, the following statements are some indicators that should raise an alarm that the prediction elements are affecting the project schedule.

"It is very complex. God willing, this task will be completed in x days."

"I am not sure, but it will be completed within a month."

"We will finish it ASAP." (means 'As Soon As Possible' but implies 'no commitment' for a project manager.)

"That should be correct, but let us double the time just in case."

"We have never done this before. Hence, it is not possible to predict when this will be done."

It is common to have timeline estimates like this for unknown aspects of a project, particularly in exploratory research and new product development. We call them 'God willing' estimates—as in, God willing, these tasks would be completed within the estimated time.

The known and unknown aspects are dealt with effectively by The Johari Window, named after its inventors Joseph Luft and Harry Ingham. It was originally developed as a model for self-awareness and personal development (Luft & Ingham, 1955). We can extrapolate the same concept for project scheduling, in a project environment that follows the four scenarios given below:

1. Known knowns
2. Known unknown
3. Unknown and Known
4. Unknown unknowns

Known knowns find a place in a project schedule with accurate time and cost estimates. Known unknowns are commonly referred to as a 'black box' and provide an appropriate provision in by way of assumptions, risks and mitigation options. The 'God willing' estimates would apply to the unknown factors, both Unknown knowns and Unknown unknowns.

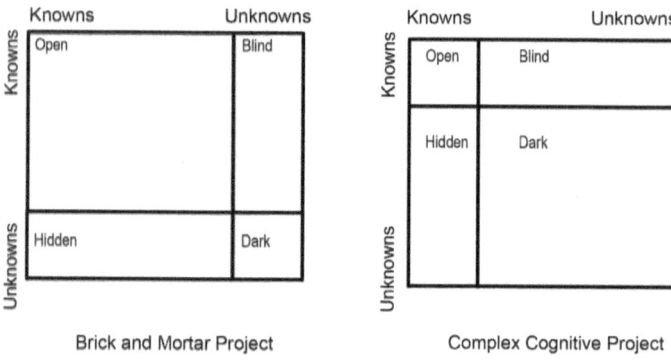

Fig 2. Johari window—applying to unknown unknown aspects of a project

It is hard to identify and estimate the time and total cost of the unknown factors at the start of a project, as these are revealed only as the project progresses. Unknown unknowns are even harder to crack, especially in new product development, innovation projects, breakthrough research or carrying out one-of-a-kind projects with no precedence.

Traditionally, project management practices attempt to deal with the unknown aspects by having contingency provisions with respect to time and cost. Ironically, even the tasks that are known upfront pose challenges when it comes to completion within the estimated time and cost—hence, completing unknown aspects with the contingency reserve is even more impractical. Trying to schedule an unknown aspect often leads to the padding of the estimates. Few project management methodologies in practice today attempt to address this, but a question that remains unanswered is of how to authenticate the accuracy of the duration of an activity and the cost.

The fact remains that the unknown factors are not adequately accounted for in any of the scheduling techniques in project management. As long as there are fewer unknown unknowns, traditional techniques will work very well but this would apply more to brick-and-mortar projects where the majority of the work depends on machines and materials. In projects such as startups, innovations, and new product development, the unknown unknowns are intensified as these kinds of projects have to deal primarily with cognitive work. In such scenarios, trying to set the project completion date accurately is like trying to pinpoint a particular place precisely on a globe. Until we get a district map and a road map, it may not be possible to do so. In the case of a map navigator, where the origin and destination are set, the directions are revealed as one starts to travel. In the event of a deviation, the navigator quickly calculates an alternate path. Likewise, we need a new way of thinking that does not target accuracy of time and cost but is flexible in its approach towards the accomplishment of the project's purpose.

Myths of managing a project

There are several conventional beliefs and practices followed by project management professionals that may seem logical at a gross level, but may be based on misconceptions inherited from the military- or industrial-age management approaches.

> *Myths of managing a project*
>
> *There are several beliefs and best practices that are followed by a project management professional every day. Some of these are commonly believed to be true and may look logical at gross level, but a subtle analysis revels them to be misconceptions inherited from Industrial age practices. These beliefs do not play a good value in the knowledge workers' era.*
>
> *Fallacy 1: The more detailed the project schedule, the better the accuracy of the project completion date.*
>
> *Fallacy 2: An average of optimistic, pessimistic and most likely estimates will lead to a realistic schedule.*
>
> *Fallacy 3: The project schedule needs to include everything that has to be done in the project.*

Fallacy 1: The more detailed the project schedule, the better the accuracy of the project completion date.

Merely having more detailed schedule does not increase the predictability of the completion date. If the task estimates are highly accurate, it will result in an accurate completion date. On the contrary, we have seen how fifty tasks of ninety percent accuracy give only 0.5 percent POS. Hence, it is not the granularity, but the accuracy of estimates that counts for predicting the completion date.

Fallacy 2: An average of the optimistic, pessimistic and nominal estimate will lead to a realistic schedule.

Probabilistic models that were useful for brick-and-mortar projects are gradually losing their usefulness in modern projects. There is no basis for a nominal estimate that explains the accuracy of the optimistic–pessimistic timeline estimates. In statistics, it is said that 'average is a misleading master.' Averaging the optimistic, pessimistic and average duration will prove to be the same when it comes to project management.

> *Fallacy 4: More resource utilization necessarily results in the project's progress.*
>
> *Fallacy 5: Whatever can go wrong will go wrong.*
>
> *Fallacy 6: Risks are undesirable for projects and to be eliminated.*
>
> *Fallacy 7: The customer is happy when the project is finished on time.*
>
> *Fallacy 8: Workaround options work.*

Fallacy 3: The project schedule needs to include everything that has to be done in the project.

Projects are progressively elaborated and, hence, there is the possibility of bringing in unknown aspects at a later stage in the lifecycle. Being prepared to undertake tasks that were not planned is critical to ensure successful completion. While beginning a project, one bound to have the tasks that are not known, that is the inherent nature of a project.

Fallacy 4: More resource utilization results in the project's progress.

Resource utilization and project progress are not necessarily directly proportional. Engaging resources to the maximum extent does not serve the purpose of the project, and does not result in progress. Also, in the case of iterative activities, only the last iteration that works would count—all other iterations would be seen as trial and error. Thus, deploying more resources does not necessarily result in progress.

Fallacy 5: Whatever can go wrong will go wrong.

The reality is that there is no right or wrong in a project—there are only planned and unforeseen tasks. When an unforeseen event occurs, it is termed as a manifestation of Murphy's Law. This is a result of not being prepared for handling unforeseen circumstances, and poor Murphy should not be accused for this.

Fallacy 6: Risks are undesirable for projects and to be eliminated.

A project is all about taking well calibrated, calculated risks. It is worth noting that high-risk projects result in higher returns and business results. Radical innovation and path-breaking products have been made possible by some companies' or individuals' appetite for risk. All that can be done is to manage the risks and exploit them to the advantage of the project.

Fallacy 7: The customer is happy when the project is finished on time.

The customer is always focused on the purpose of the project. A product that is delivered on time but has shortcomings in functionality is a greater disappointment than a product delivered late.

Fallacy 8: Workaround options work

When risk is anticipated, a contingency option or workaround option is worked out—common belief is that this should work. In reality, the Plan A or the original task itself is an uncertain one, so how would Plan B work? If there are two ways of executing a task, it means that the team is yet to figure out the best way in which the activity could be completed.

The Execution Challenge: Clock vs. Compass

Having started the project, the team steers it towards attaining the objective of creating products or services, or achieving results. The team would also report on whether the project is behind or ahead of schedule. Thus, progress is referred to in timescale terms rather than the purpose per se. Quite often, the team forgets the value they are creating, which is the very purpose of the project. There is a tendency to choose the clock over the compass.

While the clock helped project managers in the Industrial Age sail towards on-time delivery, the true north or attaining the ultimate goal plays a significant role in the Knowledge Era. Hence, today, a project manager has to balance the clock and compass for successful delivery.

The following four scenarios remind us of when we need to take a look at the compass:

1. When it is hard to define a project within the framework of time, cost and scope. It is better to begin the project with flexible project parameters but with a firm goal.

2. If a project does not have a precedent or model that can be adapted—this could lead to several

ballpark estimates while targeting for accuracy in the estimation of time. Often, we do not even use an average of optimistic, pessimistic and four times of most likely estimates to work out probable timelines for activities, but take a call on the timelines or impose a target deadline for every task.

3. When a project is progressively elaborated, it uncovers a lot of aspects that need to be resolved at later stages. Sufficient information is not available at the beginning of the project. In such cases, the time commitment one makes at the outset does not stand a chance.

4. When a customer is not able to define the user requirement clearly but comes up with a problem that needs to be solved. The vicious circle of scope change and the addition of work and amendments could mean hampering the relationship with the client at the end of the project.

The Execution Challenge: Effort and Effect

Certain projects have a direct correlation between effort and effect—these have straightforward results when the tasks are accomplished every time. The effort put in includes activities, decisions and investments, which are captured as 'tasks' in the project plan; the effect is the manifestation of the results, which results in progress towards completion.

If one wanted to consider a simple analogy, let us take the construction of a simple building. By and large, provided that the design is correct and materials are available, it can progress as per the pre-determined objectives. Every time some concrete is poured or a brick is laid, the building shall rise further. Thus, there is a clear correlation between both factors, and the effect based on effort can be clearly pre-determined.

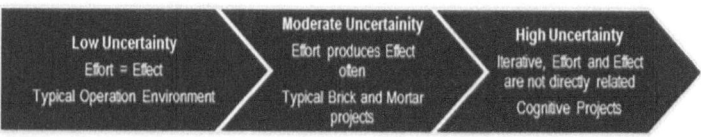

However, in some research and development (R&D) projects, this is seldom a direct correlation between effort and effect. It is said that Edison conducted a thousands of experiments to figure out a suitable filament for the electric bulb, before narrowing down on tungsten. Today, companies use the advanced design of experiments, which are aimed at reducing the number of iterations and increasing the probability of success. However, many startups, research projects and innovations are based on an iterative approach where effect and effort are not directly proportional. It often takes multiple iterations to get the desired results, and to set the path right. Every iteration does not help the project progress. However, a project schedule aims to have tasks lined up one after another—which are essentially efforts—and expects progress against each of these tasks in return.

Flawless planning with high precision is possible for a project that has a clear correlation between effort and effect. Time, scope and cost can be accurately pre-determined for such projects. When there is no direct correlation between effort and effect, it's hard to determine the precise time and cost factors.

The Gap: Estimation, Commitment and Delivery

In a project lifecycle, the ability to ascertain parameters such as cost and time are at their least at the beginning of the project. Ironically this is where the estimates are worked out. The commitments (for scope, budget and timelines) needed for projects are provided close to the beginning of the project once the calculations are worked out. As the project progresses, the ability to forecast increases, but as the commitments are made upfront, the team is bound by these projections. The gap between the estimate at the start of the project and the actuals at the end of the project reflects the ability of the team to forecast the parameters accurately. A smaller gap results in better anticipation and lineup of budget and resources for seamless execution. A bigger gap results in scope creeps, time delays and budget escalations to bring the project under control and achieve the stated objectives.

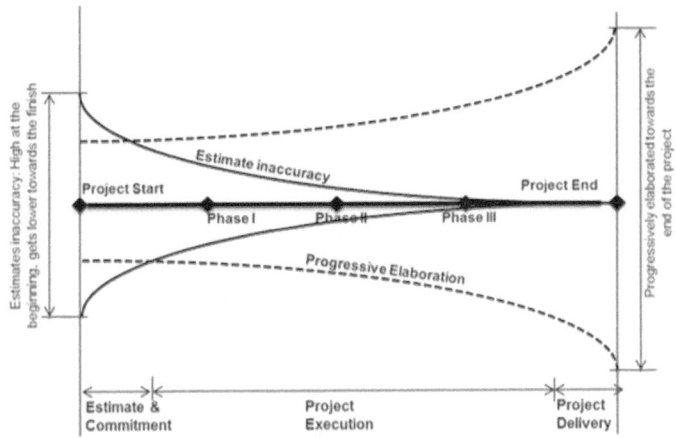

Fig 3. Estimate, commitment and delivery in deterministic model

Traditional project management practices try to address the gap between commitment and actuals through contingency reserves. This helps to a certain extent but does not protect the project entirely if the deviation is beyond a reasonable limit anticipated at the beginning. There is an element of guesswork based on past experience for working out the contingency reserve. The accuracy of the estimate depends on the accuracy of these collective experiences and this does not guarantee the ability of the reserve to fully bridge the gap. *Traditional practices are, thus, designed for scope creeps, cost escalations and timeline deviations.*

The progressive elaboration could bring in opportunities as well as threats, which could advance or delay a project. While the contingency provisions address most of the negative aspects, the opportunities are not dealt with. This is an important factor that affects the viability of today's projects, as *the speed at which the product is brought to market is a key criterion for success.*

Part 2

The changing paradigm of project management

Businesses realize that there is a need for a shift in project management practices. Factors that reinforce this need include:

The need to increase the speed of projects and product developments are necessitated by the shorter lifecycle of products and faster rate of product obsolescence.

1. Competitive forces influence the viability of projects, which require more agile and nimble decisions.
2. The shift in the workforce from industrial laborers to knowledge workers, which requires a flexible framework that enables cognitive work and ensures focus on the purpose of the project.
3. The rigid project practices stifle the cognitive nature of the work. Deadlines and time pressure work against creative thinking and innovation, which are part of a breakthrough research environment.

While the necessity is felt, the following factors impede change:

1. It is convenient to confine a project to the time, cost and scope framework.
2. Though uncertainty is an inherent part of projects, traditional practices offer a fixed scope, cost estimate and strict deadline, which enables ease of accounting and business planning.

3. Customers, both internal and external, understand deadlines and pre-determined costs more quickly. Often, the client evaluates the project only after delivery and requests for changes only if it does not meet the expectations.

Multiple models have already emerged as alternatives to traditional project management practices.

Modern project management had originated, as we've seen, with an interest in scheduling and cost control techniques but then developed as a means of coordination. (Morris, 2013)

While the above factors demonstrate the need for a change in the way in which projects are managed, we are also seeing that the emerging trends in project management are skewed towards the purpose-centric model. Purpose-centric models can provide an enabling framework that can improve knowledge workers' motivation, and foster involvement and engagement in the creative process.

The Ultimate Shift: From triple constraints to the purpose

The well-known parable of an emperor wearing an 'invisible' suit explains how following other people's opinions blindly can lead us to misconceptions. Let us look at the way in which the tasks are planned, coordinated, executed and controlled in projects. Time, cost and scope are the only factors used to measure a project progress. These are certainly important parameters but fail to address the core intent.

The ultimate question is whether time, cost and scope—the triple constraints—are more important than fulfilling the project's purpose.

Scope: A customer may not be able to define the scope initially, but he/she may have a hazy idea of what needs to be done. Keeping this as a starting point means that the scope of the project is defined loosely. If change is seen as a billing opportunity but, eventually, it will hurt the business-client relationship. Instead of opting for a rigid scope definition and multiple changes, why not define the underlying purpose in the first place?

Time: There are various parts of a project that are iterative by nature. They can be used to provide a reasonable prediction for operations like jobs, but not for R&D or cognitive jobs.

Cost: If the time and scope cannot be predicted accurately, determination of cost will also be inaccurate. If the initial cost calculation is misleading, the viability of the entire project is questionable.

The underlying assumption is that the tasks that exceed the time and cost would be compensated for by those that finish ahead of timeline and consume less cost. In reality, while the delays are passed on, the advancements are not. Work expands to the available time, and is often not delivered earlier than scheduled. Even in cases where early delivery is feasible, the stakeholder located downstream is unprepared to take up the task early.

The triangular model of cost, time and scope show only parameters that are to be measured but not the ultimate objectives. Surgery is a good analogy of a real-world project. It is a broad category of invasive medical treatments for specific reasons. Every surgery is unique and has definite start and end. If a surgeon were given projects with fixed cost, time and scope, and his key performance indicators were based on this, what would happen? In reality, many surgeries go beyond textbook models. A surgeon takes stock of the situation on hand and makes decisions based on his (and his team's) wisdom. The only critical parameter is the purpose of the surgery—which is the patient's wellness. Time, cost and scope have to be flexible, and directed towards the ultimate purpose. Though the diagnosis is made upfront, there are limitations as to what can be seen before uncovering the affected area during the surgery. The surgeon then makes necessary adjustments based on how the patient is responding. This is a good metaphor for why projects need to be purpose-driven rather than time-focused.

As in the example given above, having the customer in mind could help businesses overcome several issues with regard to project failures. While the customers want the project to be delivered on time, they care about how it adds value to their businesses or lives. Often, the project goes to a 'point of no return' where the customer needs this project as a part of a major program that is a vital component of a strategy. Sometimes the customer has already paid for the product/service and is patiently waiting for it. In such cases, when there is a deviation from the initially estimated scope, additional funds and time are provided as long as the project is able to deliver the core purpose of the project. This is because the undying value can be still achieved by the project and it is still inherently available in the project.

If the purpose of the project is the target, it needs to be measured and relied on for all decisions. On the contrary, project managers generally consider the variables as the target. While the world progressed from the Industrial Age to the Information Age, the project management community hung on to the old mindset and applied the same to new projects as well.

Paradigm shift of projects from Industrial Age to Knowledge Era

Systems such as PERT or GANTT were originally developed for purposes that apply to industrial and military applications. These may not be relevant for projects that we are currently working on. In the Knowledge Era, there are several other factors that will engage the workforce.

Our current business operating system–which is built around external, carrot-and-stick motivators–doesn't work and often does harm. We need an upgrade. And the science shows the way. This new approach has three essential elements: 1. Autonomy – the desire to direct our own lives. 2. Mastery – the urge to get better and better at something that matters. 3. Purpose – the yearning to do what we do in the service of something larger than ourselves: (Pink D. H., 2008)

Every shift in the human race—from hunter-gatherers to the information Age—has proven that productivity has increased significantly, by over a hundred times. In the Information Era, projects deliver value that is several times that of those in the Industrial Age. The use of techniques developed for Industrial-era projects undermines the capability of the knowledge worker to deliver according to expectations. In today's world we don't call them 'workers' but 'associates' and 'partners.'

	Hunters and Gatherers	Agricultural Age	Industrial Age	Information Age
Workforce	Hunters	Farmers	Factory workers	Knowledge workers
Skillset	Strength	Strength Forecasting Tactics Systematic	Specialist Discipline	Intellect Creativity
Mindset	Survival of the fittest	Organized Community living, Assertiveness	Leadership and followership	Passion Volunteer ship DIY
Tools	Hunting tools	Farming Tools	Machines Systems Automation	Information Innovation Internet
Focus	Need of the hour	Independence	Efficiency Effectiveness	Purpose Value Creativity Interdependence
Management	Survival	Manage Control Discipline	Lead, Command and Control	Inspire, Unleash Adapt
Productivity	Baseline	Multiple times than hunters and gatherers	Multiple times than farmers	Multiple times than factory workers

(Contd.)

SPIRAL STAIRCASE PROJECT MANAGEMENT

	Hunters and Gatherers	Agricultural Age	Industrial Age	Information Age
Motivation	Food Survival	Community living Being in control	Targets, Rewards Recognition Carrot-and-Stick	Purpose Equity Ownership Making a difference Shared Vision
Ecosystem	Individual Family	Family Community	Pyramid consist of laborers, employees, leaders and followers	Intrapreneurs Partners Associates
Projects	Hunting projects	Farming and building shelters	Industrial projects Megastructures	Radical Cognitive Innovation projects
Products	Food	Food, safety and security	Meet market needs with useful products Mass production	Create markets with specialty products
Failure tolerance	Errors cost life	Errors challenge survival	Accurate delivery FTR MTBF	Iterative processes Encouraged to make mistakes

	Hunters and Gatherers	Agricultural Age	Industrial Age	Information Age
Engagement	Individual Groups	Manpower	Hands	Head, heart and hands
Project assets	Strength	Bloodline	Guideline Checklist	Network Knowledge
Project Schedules	Ad-hoc Natural laws	Informal, Determined by strength of individual and groups	Determined by machines' speed and performance	Speed of mind Decision-making Collaboration

Fig 4: *Table: Project ecosystem of various ages*

There is also the emergence of the Conceptual Age as indicated by Dan Pink in his book, 'A Whole New Mind: Why Right-Brainers Will Rule the Future' (Pink, 2006), which demonstrates that the creators and empathizers will rule the world, going forward.

Thomas Alva Edison is regarded as the creator of the first industrial research laboratory. What if Edison considered his making of the incandescent electric bulb as a 'project'? As per our project management practices, it would have been termed a failure and would have been closed long before he would have 'seen the light.' In today's context, several startups begin with a flexible framework and progressively elaborated over time. Take, for example, Facebook, when it was founded as a startup. If Mark Zuckerberg waited for a project charter with accurate estimate of time, cost and scope upfront, it would not have become what it is today. Likewise, many startups today have a clearly defined purpose or the direction in which it needs to progress, however they need flexibility in the time, cost and scope aspects. This approach allows the projects to unleash their potential and helps them reach their ultimate goal. However, the underlying need is to have a clear, unambiguous purpose, which will stand as the true north of the project.

Characteristics of an Information Era project

Like a spiral staircase, a project in today's environment becomes progressively elaborated and needs to undertake many steps to accomplish its purpose. Also, there is seldom a direct link between effort and effect. Hence, trying to fix precise timeline becomes a challenging task.

An Information Era project has more cognitive dependency. Earlier, projects depended on the equipment to do their job—today, it banks upon minds to create the results. As the human minds create a project in this era, the efficiency of a project is determined by how best the human resources work and how motivated they are. Hence, a sense of ownership, a shared vision and passion are needed. In the Industrial Age, well-oiled machines are required in order to perform effectively; in the Information Age, the human mind has to be enabled with ownership and involvement to perform the tasks better. Hence, a volunteer workforce is the key to success.

Finally, the external environment has a greater influence on project feasibility and viability and the lifecycle of products after their launch. Hence, there is a need for a project management framework that addresses all these elements—a method that can enable rather than restrict.

Transforming triple constraints to triple opportunities

The triple constraints is an intelligible algorithm to relate to the cost, time and scope of a project and is still relevant for many projects where these aspects needs to be controlled. It gives varying degrees of success and entirely depends on whether one can calculate these three parameters precisely at the start of the project. This triangle can be a very useful tool for controlling an Industrial Age project. Traditional project management practices hover around control of these parameters. The entire analytical framework we have today is based on this trade-off. It is important to have upfront visibility of all these three parameters to use this algorithm effectively. At the outset, for disruptive, radical innovation projects, where upfront computation of these parameters is not viable, controlling this triangle is not feasible. Also, one can control only what is measured. If the accuracy of the measurement itself is under question, controlling the project is not possible.

The triple constraints algorithm disregards the capabilities of the people that executed and delivers project tasks. It assumes that a standard amount of time is required for delivering a scope of work by utilizing the estimated cost. In reality, however, this is applicable only to machines. For intellectual work, we know that the output varies from resource to resource, based on competencies. Research shows that a high performer can be 400 percent more productive than an average performer (O'BOYLE JR., 2013). Likewise, in a project, a highly capable and inspired scientist or engineer can deliver much more in a given time by utilizing the same amount of resources for the same task. This is the very reason why triple constraints are irrelevant for knowledge workforce.

For cognitive projects, we need to see the other side of this triangle—we call it 'the opportunity side of the triangle.' The purpose of measuring time is to complete the project at the earliest. If the computation of a timeline is a problem for cognitive projects, the focus needs to be shifted to the speed or velocity of the activities in the direction of completing the project at the earliest. The purpose of cost control is to ensure that the project is completed within optimum investment. The other side of cost control is to make sure that every penny spent on the project is worthy, and creates value for the client or sponsor. The purpose of scope is to see that the project is aligned with the pre-determined work packages in the interest of completing the project—the other dimension of achieving the same is to see it does not deviate from the project's purpose.

There is tremendous potential for project teams to hone a new way of working by flipping the approach to improving each of these aspects rather than controlling them, particularly when they are unknown or partially known, as is the case in cognitive projects.

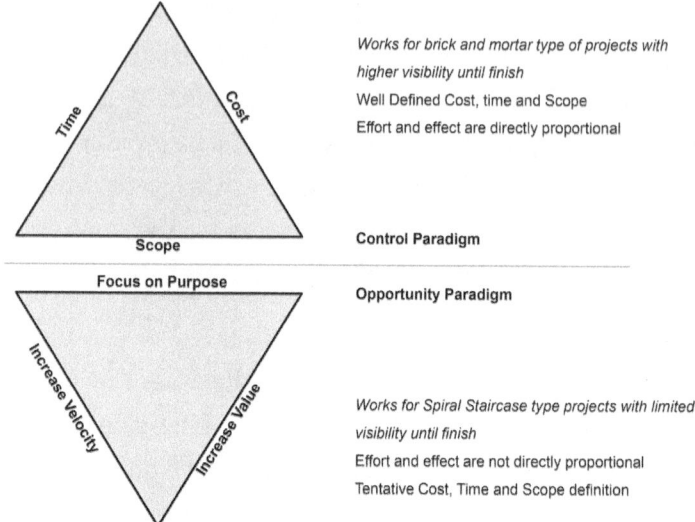

Fig 5: Transforming triple constraints from control paradigm to opportunity paradigm

Time: Transforming deadline to velocity

Traditional project management advocates a target date for project completion, and the entire team works towards it. All activities are organized in a logical sequence to derive the overall project duration. The project's success or failure depends on the team's ability to meet this target. In research projects, this can't be determined accurately upfront. Hence, instead of controlling time, the focus needs to be shifted to increasing the velocity of every step. The speed of an individual step determines the speed of the whole project, which determines the total duration of the project. This is like a relay race, where the speed of the individual runner who holds the baton determines the speed of the entire team. Increasing the velocity of every individual step is an opportunity to reduce the overall timeline. This, in turn, results in faster delivery. This also has the edge over deterministic models as the time estimate for the activities itself is questionable. Moreover, aspects such as Student Syndrome or Parkinson's Law can be preempted by focusing on improving the velocity of every step. (Student Syndrome refers to a tendency to procrastinate until the deadline of a project; Parkinson's Law states that the work expands to fill the available time.)

Velocity imperatives: Some of the systematic changes in the project ecosystem would lead to an enabling environment to increase the velocity of a cognitive project. Consider some velocity maximizers from the examples provided below:

a. Clear decisions that enable advancement of project without interruptions

b. A highly capable and inspired workforce completes the tasks faster

c. Accountability and responsibility are clearly defined, in pursuance of avoiding ambiguity

d. Involvement of the execution team enables passionate execution of projects

e. Working out watertight schedules for activities that are visible

f. Upfront definitions of way forward are given in the case of 'if-else' scenarios to avoid ambiguity

g. Mono-tasking to improve speed of delivery of every task

h. Mono-tasking to improve delivery and prevent changeover time

i. Clear communication and collaboration

j. Avoidance of communication crusade that saps time and energy of resources

k. Enabling reduction in iterations

l. Defining turn around times (TAT) for every interface and increasing service levels

m. Improved integration between work streams to reinforce interdependency

n. Expert groups or subject matter experts (SMEs) for specific jobs for focused, faster delivery

o. Not idling for the input material

p. Decentralization: teams are empowered to take decision

q. Availability of bench strength or additional resources in case of need

Every project has two types of activities—namely, efforts and idle time. In a project schedule, efforts are referred as tasks. This can be further classified into two categories—one that results in the progress of the project, and the other which does not add to progress. The former has the effort-effect correlation while the latter does not. Some of the iterative efforts in research projects are not converted as results—hence, these will fall under the latter. However, they are necessary to move towards a final iteration that is required for progress in the project.

Idle time can also be classified into types—namely, forced idle time and planned idle time. Forced idle time includes analytical test results, which are time-bound. Such idle time is inevitable and one has to wait in order to get to the next activity to start. The second type, planned idle time, depends on the nature of the project schedule. This includes waiting for other activities to be completed in order to proceed to next activity. A project schedule consists of a series of these four types of activities. The overall velocity of projects can be increased through effective planning. Effectiveness in the plan can be brought in by working out a watertight project schedule that is designed to consist (predominantly) of the tasks that enable the project's progress. This can be achieved by building a schedule such that idle time is covered by parallel activities that help the project's progress. Using this technique can also contribute to minimize tasks that do not add to the project's progress, and thereby improve velocity. Changeover time reduction between tasks and seamless handover between one work stream and another are factors that will improve the velocity of the project. Having a watertight schedule, transparent decision-making, and a passionate engaging workforce indeed results in improvement of the velocity of the overall project.

Cost: Transforming controlling cost to maximizing value

In the deterministic model, the cost of the project is derived by summing up the costs of all individual tasks, materials, men, machines and the methods needed to deliver each activity successfully. In research projects, cost estimates calculated upfront are seldom accurate. This is not only because of unpredictability, but also due to the number of iterations that have to be tried to deliver a step. The lack of correlation between effect and effort also makes it difficult to predict the cost. Hence, instead of controlling the cost, the approach needs to center on maximizing the project's value from each and every step. The dictionary definition of 'value' is the worth of all the benefits and rights arising from ownership. This can be accomplished in two ways: First, by increasing the quality of the products or service; second, by improving the utility of the products or services. Hence, the approach in the cognitive project is to look for opportunities for maximizing the value of each and every step through creating more benefits to the customer for every dollar spent.

Value imperatives: The following are some examples of the value maximizing imperatives in a project environment:

   a. Reduction in the number of iterations, and passing on of the cost advantage to the customer or sponsor
   b. Use of latest technologies in the project and elimination of obsolescence; use of latest materials, methods and knowledge

c. Improving quality of delivery at every step, which improves the quality of the project as a whole

d. Improved focus to improve the product's core purpose rather than working on ancillary benefits

e. Failing early and, thus, failing cheap—identification and pruning of unviable projects at early stages.Use of economies of scale to reduce cost

f. Better utilization of capacities in the interest of obtaining optimum returns from available project resources

g. Use of SMEs to maximize the value of individual steps

h. Increased productivity from resources committed to project

i. Reducing total cost of ownership

One of the best expressions I have learned about cost optimization is: "Today's project teams have a lot of money to spend but none to waste." This is a profound message—we should invest every dollar in the project tasks that results in the progress of the project and, ultimately, in the improvement of value for the customer.

Scope: Transforming rigid scope definition to what it needs to deliver

In deterministic models, the scope is worked out by adding all that is necessary to deliver the project based on the upfront estimate. In cases of ambiguity, the scope statement is referred to, to see the demarcation between what is in-scope and out-of-scope. The list of assumption, risks and workaround options are also worked out upfront. The scope also specifies who will have to bear the cost in case of a deviation. Quite often, in a typical project scope statement, risk manifestations are written on the part of the customer. In other words, all that is presumed to be necessary to deliver the project is included in the project scope. However, in order to avoid scope creep, everything needs to go right the first time itself. If any unanticipated tasks are to be done, it is charged to the customer. In a research project, seldom does everything go right the first time. When things do not go as expected, scope creep and change management come into play. All this, in turn, reduces the speed of the project and results in cumbersome ad-hoc decisions, approval and paperwork. In other words, with a conventional, rigid scope framework, one is not prepared for doing all that is needed but for all that is perceived as necessary in the initial planning stage. Preparation for unplanned tasks and harnessing of unfolding possibilities, and responding to these developments agile is a key differentiator in today's world. Hence, instead of sticking to a rigid scope, holding to the purpose is the shift that is needed for cognitive projects. Laser-sharp focus on the objectives will help the team remain adaptable and responsible for delivering the same. Even traditionally, this was achieved through scope creep at the end of the day—hence, being prepared for this helps avoids going through bureaucratic scope creeps and change control processes that slow down the project's pace.

Purpose imperatives: The following are some examples of imperatives that enable focus on purpose rather than a rigid scope framework:

   a. Fostering purpose-centric project ecosystems
   b. Clear, unambiguous definition of the purpose of the project and a roadmap to achieve the same
   c. Focus on the purpose of the project at every stage of the project—all other attributes are either input to the project or additional outcomes; consistent recalibration of project course to align it with the purpose
   d. Harnessing unfolding opportunities due to technological development, and handling unplanned tasks due to progressive elaboration
   e. Focusing on developing high-quality products, services or results Responding to internal and external development that might hamper the project
   f. Focusing on the true north and not on parameters
   g. Engagement of center of excellence
   h. Uncomplicated scope change practices that make changes possible, if needed
   i. Make bench strength and contingent investment accessible to project teams, if necessary
   j. Focused mini project teams with clear accountability and faster decisions

k. Incentives and KPIs being aligned with the purpose of the project
l. Leveraging eureka moments to benefit from it for projects
m. Fostering the creative process for the sake of gaining maximum benefit from it

From desperation to inspiration

Traditionally, it has been believed that projects are to be controlled through time, cost and resource utilization. Earned value management was one of the best approaches to accomplish this in industrial-age projects. Sailing an S-curve becomes necessary in such cases. However, the challenge in the cognitive project is not limited to sailing the S-curve, but in beating the product life cycle and technological obsolesce and getting ahead of the fierce competition. If measurement drives behavior, it is obvious that when the team is measured against time, cost and scope, they are motivated to control cost and time and to work on the framework of scope. Their desperation to meet these pre-determined parameters takes precedence over anything else. In R&D projects, due to their complex nature, and the fact that the project's primary driver is the human mind, the approach is to look beyond these constraints. Engaging the heads, hearts and hands of the team and unleashing their talent is the right approach. This is accomplished by making the project resources the owners of the project. The environment is made more conducive, so that they have a sense of ownership and enthusiasm. Hence, intrapreneurs and volunteers are needed to carry out today's R&D projects. The employees' mindset will bring in results, but superior results can be gotten only by inspired minds that are connected to a larger purpose. Businesses need to cultivate inspiration model in the interest of benefiting from the knowledge workforce of today while executing cognitive projects. Many aspects, such as mono-tasking and having a clear vision of the projects, are imperative in enhancing velocity, value and purpose. The new approach, illustrated in subsequent chapters, tries to address most of them.

Part 3

A new framework for today's cognitive projects

Staircase and Project Management

At the outset, a question that comes up is of the link between staircases and project management. For the sake of simplicity, let us refer to a well-known definition of projects:

A project is a temporary endeavor undertaken to create a unique product, service, or result. (PMBOK, A Guide To The Project Management Body Of Knowledge, 5th ed., 2015)

A project is progressively elaborated, but has a definite start and definite finish and creates unique products that have not been created so far. If a typical production endeavor had variability as a challenge, a typical project endeavor has uncertainty (along with variability) as a challenge. Project management methodologies have recommended several ways to resolve this. Every project management framework has its own approach in determining precise timelines so as to deliver the product or services within budget. There are several kinds of project controls used to ensure that the project is accomplished as per the plan.

Spiral staircase is a metaphor used to illustrate the construct of a cognitive project. Like a spiral staircase, in a project, few steps are visible at the beginning—as the project progresses, more and more steps are revealed. This is also known as 'progressively elaborated' in the project management fraternity. In an ideal scenario, if there are no issues in any of the steps, the project progresses seamlessly as per the plan. In a project or in a spiral staircase, one knows the target destination and some of the intermediate levels to be crossed in order to reach the destination with further more details of the steps, which are visible from the starting point.

With the available visibility, project schedules are prepared. In the beginning, as is the case of the spiral staircase, there are many steps for which the details are not known but these are included in the schedule with several assumptions. A contingency in the budget and buffer in the schedule is provided to protect the project against any manifestation of risks and issues.

A staircase is a structure made for taking people from one place to another place. It has a beginning and a destination. Like a staircase, products or services are created by going through various steps in a project. These are called work packages, and consist of tasks, activities or Work Breakdown Structure (WBS), in project management textbooks.

Let us look at the types of staircases and their relevance to projects. For the purpose of this book, three kinds of staircases are being considered as a metaphor to projects:

1. Linear staircase
2. Spiral staircase
3. Circular staircase

A linear staircase consists of a set of symmetrical steps leading from one level to another. All the steps in a linear staircase can be seen from the starting point. This provides greater visibility of a number of steps and intermediate platforms to cross before reaching the final destination.

The rise and run of the individual steps are known at the beginning of the staircase. There are no surprises as one sees all the steps vividly. If one goes up this staircase, it takes him to the destination. Many projects are like this linear staircase. All the tasks are predictable, and can be visualized at the planning stage itself. There are hidden risks or opportunities that are not revealed at the beginning. This offers less of a challenge in managing the project. One knows that traveling through each of the steps will take us a level up, and finally in reaching the destination or delivering the products or services of the project. In such projects, efficiency plays a vital role in advancing through the staircase at a rapid pace. The schedule can be as granular as possible, and defining time, cost and resource needs with high levels of accuracy are entirely possible. The probability of achieving these steps right the first time and every time is also high.

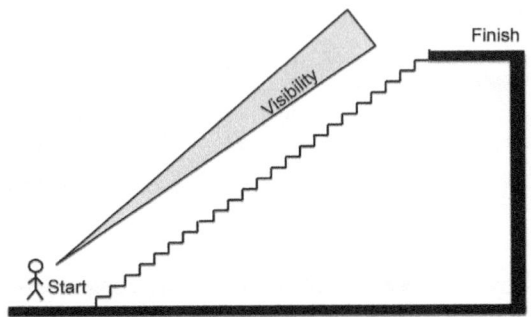

Fig 6: Linear Staircase Metaphor and Visibility of Steps Ahead

A spiral staircase, also on the other hand, has several steps to get through to reach a destination. Also, it offers visibility of only a few steps that are close to the beginning.

The subsequent steps are revealed only after the particular flight has been traveled. There are several projects in today's context that are like the spiral staircase. All that is known is the destination, which needs to be reached, or the purpose of the project, and very few steps that have to be carried out at the start. Many of the activities, which have to be performed in the future, are known only approximately or remain unknown, but they are revealed as the project progresses.

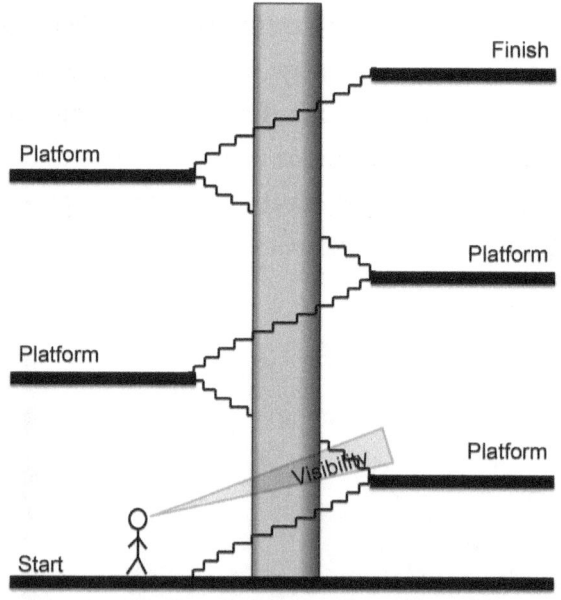

Fig 7: Spiral Staircase Metaphor and Visibility of Steps Ahead

A circular staircase is a hybrid of linear and spiral staircases. It has several linear staircases one after another, placed in a circular shape. It offers more visibility when compared to a spiral staircase but is not as vivid as a linear staircase. This is a metaphor for certain types of projects as well. The approach used for spiral staircase projects would apply to circular ones as well.

A staircase that inspired me and kindled the thinking of comparing a spiral staircase to a project is at the Koln Cathedral. When I visited Germany, I had a small window of opportunity to see the south tower with a twenty-four-ton, largest free-swinging bell in the world. The spiral staircase leads the way to the top of the Cologne Cathedral. The tower is 475 feet high, and 533 steps take visitors to the 332-feet-high landing. Walking through this staircase is a real example of progressive elaboration of a project, where every step is unrevealed as one embarks the journey towards the top of the tower. There are very impressive and inspiring structures, around the world. My recommendation for you is to relate to the concept of project progress when you happen to climb a spiral staircase next time.

If a project does have limited visibility of the steps to be undertaken in order to deliver the products or services, the team will face several challenges in planning and delivering the products or services with precision. In subsequent chapters, these aspects are evaluated in details and this simple metaphor surprisingly paves the way for an alternate framework for effective project planning and execution.

Spiral Staircase and Project Management

Fig 8: Visibility of steps in a spiral staircase

Challenges in Management of Projects

Year on year, research and surveys are undertaken to measure and publish the success and failure of projects in various sectors. Studies done by prominent consulting firms a decade ago on the success rate of projects show that a significant percentage of projects are unsuccessful—in terms of not meeting the goal of completing the project within the given time, scope and cost. These surveys were done decades ago—and the situation has not changed much even today. A study conducted by McKinsey and the BT Centre for Major Programme Management at the University of Oxford, on more than 5,400 information technology (IT) projects, show that, on average, large IT projects run forty-five percent over budget and seven percent over time, while delivering fifty-six percent less value than predicted (Michael Bloch, 2012). Major factors that contributed to these failures, in descending order are: a) unclear objectives, b) unrealistic schedule c) shifting requirement and technical complexity, and d) unaligned team.

Practically speaking, the project-driven environment in every organization evidences the challenges faced in delivering projects successfully.

One common denominator in all these statistics is that time was referred to as the success criteria of the project across the globe. With this definition and analytical framework, half the projects are classified as 'failed.' Apparently, failure refers to the lack of compliance with cost, time and scope. On average, around sixty percent of the projects undergo scope change.

Such small probabilities usually do not attract more and continued interest or investment. Despite this fact, many projects are kicked off every year. There are three primary reasons for the ongoing interest in spite of disheartening statistics on the failure rate of projects:

- Firstly, all projects termed as 'failures' are not necessarily actual failures—they are only unable to meet the analytical framework used as a measurement of success. The accuracy of the upfront definition of these factors also determines the success or failure of the project. If the accuracy of the parameters is incorrect, defining success based on them is inappropriate. This only demonstrates the failure of the analytical framework to measure the success or failure of the project and not the project itself.

- Secondly, even if a project is said to have failed with respect to the definition of time, cost and scope, the value it can provide to the customer might be inherent. That why many projects are continued, even if they are not completed on time, within budget and in scope. When the project delivers its value, its purpose is accomplished and it becomes truly successful.

- Thirdly, the original scope defined is not in accordance with the purpose of the project—and this is revealed in due course, when necessary adjustments are made in pursuance of achieving the purpose. In this process, preset KPIs or analytical framework are no longer valid as a measure of success.

Businesses must re-examine the way in which projects are measured and evaluated, as this would require a paradigm shift in order to track the real success of projects. A purpose-centric definition of project scope eliminates poor scope estimate, and directly connects to the customer's needs. I had the opportunity to execute, manage and lead hundreds of projects over the last two decades. The projects were for various organizations, which has varied levels of project management maturity and with different cultural environments. These projects were key strategic and business efforts—be it a development of new products or creation of capacity. These projects always ended up as a mixed bag of success and failures. My inference is that not all projects that are termed as 'failures' are real failures. A fraction of them did not make it through, but several projects that were completed later than planned had scope creep but managed to meet their purpose. One of the projects I can quote as an illustration for the purpose-centric approach is that of a drug development project for a pharmaceutical company. The project consisted of the development of an active ingredient called Gabapentin (for the treatment of epilepsy), and the construction of a facility to manufacture the drug substance. We faced several hurdles during execution, due to progressively elaborated aspects, and the project was not completed on time. According to the definition of project management, it fell behind all estimated parameters. However, a few months later than the initially targeted finish date, the team developed a cost-efficient, high-quality drug, commissioned the plant and was able to manufacture the product. This product became a major part of the company's portfolio and went on to become a best-seller. The company also expanded the product by vertical integration. When I look back at the project after a decade, I would certainly consider it a success, even though it did not comply with the pre-determined timeframe. It made a significant contribution to the top line and bottom-line growth of the company. More importantly, this product continues to make its contribution in providing affordable healthcare for millions of patients.

Hence, by making the purpose non-negotiable and making the time, cost and quality flexible, one can make the delivery model more suited to today's projects. Moreover, this approach connects the project to the customers, who need to receive the pre-determined value from the project. This also strengthens the project algorithm, as it is aligned with the core purpose. The needed shift in the approach is from pre-determined cost, time and scope to the purpose and value creation of a project.

Spiral Staircase Explained

The purpose of spiral staircase project management:

In the information era, cognitive projects and their intricacies cannot be framed within the triangle of cost, time and scope. There is a need for a methodology that will enable the project team to carryout a project with an increase in overall velocity. Spiral Staircase Project Management (SSPM) aims to increase overall velocity by focusing on the flow of the project. It offers the needed flexibility and makes the project agile and nimble, and to be prepared for handling the progressively elaborated aspects of a typical information era project.

Let us get into the architecture of a spiral staircase in more detail in order to understand the methodology. A spiral staircase is a structure constructed around a central axis or a newel, which goes from a level to another in a building. The height of the staircase, from the starting point to the destination, is called 'total rise.' Throughout the total rise, in the case of a multi-floor construction, large spiral staircases are provided with additional, intermediate landings. These intermediate landings or platforms are provided to facilitate a change in direction, access to multiple floors or landing places. These platforms divide the large staircase into several sections that lead to the intermediate levels through the platforms. A fleet is a consecutive series of steps from one platform to another.

At the beginning of the spiral staircase, the entire set of steps leading to the destination is not visible. All that is visible is the first few steps or a fleet until the next platform. After going through these steps, the next fleet becomes visible, and the more one travels through the staircase, the more steps are revealed and, ultimately, the final destination. Beyond the immediate next steps, there are other steps that can be seen from the bottom of the steps, handrail, newel and supports.

When it comes to considering a spiral staircase as a metaphor for projects, we may not have to visualize a perfectly intact staircase. A project spiral staircase is not a perfectly intact, monolithic structure but one with a lot of uncertainties and surprises. Like a spiral staircase, in a project environment, as we see the number of floors and the destination at the beginning, what is clearly defined is the goal, and the intermittent stages that the project needs to go through to achieve its objectives. However, the details of each step are often not vividly known at the beginning. Depending on the type of project, greater visibility of the further steps is possible. Several future steps can be identified from a different dimension, such as from the bottom of the top fleet, which is visible from a level below. However, this does not give exact details and intricacies of the steps available ahead in the projects until one reaches that stage. Until then, one could undertake the journey, assuming that what has been seen from a different dimension could be true.

In a 'project spiral staircase,' in addition to steps that are not known at the beginning, there are several steps may be weak and there could be missing steps as well. Detailing everything with hundred percent precision is not possible at the beginning of the project. There are certain aspects that are revealed only after the project progresses to a certain extent. Often, the only way to get to know the actual attributes of an additional step is to go through the earlier steps and reach that stage. A project management staircase is one that requires all imperfections to be corrected and missing steps to be constructed as one goes from the beginning to the end. There are steps that are rusty, which have lost their connection with the base, and sometimes repeated in subsequent steps. In projects, some steps were never conceived in the initial stages. The initial estimate of efforts for some steps would eventually require some additional repairs while crossing the steps—read this as scope creep. The resources and cost needed for this would be higher than initial estimates. If the risk and response planning are robust, the project moves smoothly. Ironically, there are some positive aspects as well but we would not know of them at the start of the project. They are known only when one goes past the early stages.

Likewise, in a project, we have clear visibility on what is to be achieved in the short term. One can come up with a detailed plan for these activities. There are some tasks that we know we need to perform but may not have visibility on how they are going to be performed, and what is required for us to complete them. There are some tasks that we know slightly from a different angle, but not know what they look like exactly.

As long as one is aware of the purpose that needs to be delivered, we can come up with a schedule that includes the major steps. The immediate steps can be calculated with precision, but all the effort put into detailing the tasks that are 'progressively elaborated' may be inaccurate. Under such circumstances, a high-level plan will do the purpose as long as it is connected to the overall objective. Just as we know that going through a fleet of the spiral staircase has to take up to next level, we also know every fleet in a project will take us closer to the intended purpose of the project.

Foundation Principles

> *We can't solve problems by using the same kind of thinking we used when we created them.*
>
> Albert Einstein

Spiral Staircase Project Management is a progressive project management framework that aims to co-create a larger project through several interdependent mini projects, with multiple expert groups processing each of these sections. Seven foundation principles upon which the SSPM framework is constructed.

Principle 1: Progressively elaborated projects are progressively planned

Calculating time, cost and scope upfront, while having many aspects unclear at the beginning, leads to incorrect estimates. If pre-determined scope, time and cost are used as the criteria for success or failure, or used as an analytical framework to measure the progress of the project, it could lead to chaos. Progressive elaboration is an inherent characteristic of a project, and things unfold as the project progresses. Hence, time, cost and scope should be calculated at various intervals for every section of the project, as the project progresses. Hence, the estimates are accurate when calculated after the different aspects are made clear, and just before the execution of the respective sections. Thus, in SSPM, progressively elaborated projects are progressively planned. However, there is a need for a high-level estimate at the beginning of every project, in order to line up resources. Spiral Staircase Project Management focuses on enabling tremendous potential by creating opportunities for increasing velocity, enhancing value and focusing on the purpose instead of controlling deterministic cost, scope and time.

Principle 2: The purpose of the project is the most important goal

The purpose is the very reason for the project's existence. Time, cost and scope are some of the indicators of achieving the project's goal but they are not the ultimate goal. Hence, delivery of purpose is SSPM's aim rather than meeting attributes of a project. Merely meeting the analytical framework of time, cost and scope of a project do not guarantee that the purpose of the project can be fulfilled. While the analytical framework is relevant for measuring the 'progress' of the project, the project's 'success' is determined by the ability of the project to attain its purpose. Businesses must realize that the probability of deviating from a project's original scope, time and cost does exist in a real-world scenario and hence it needs to build flexibility for these attributes in the interest of achieving the purpose of the project. The ultimate objective of a project is to deliver the purpose the project it is intended to create.

Principle 3: Assumptions can go wrong

Assumptions are a means by which Industrial Age projects dealt with unknowns. Ironically, the estimates of time, scope and cost do not factor in these assumptions—they are almost like a disclaimer. In the case of wrong assumptions, the project often needs additional funding or extension of deadline. The assumptions are often used as justification of why the projects are not delivered according to pre-determined targets. In real life, seldom do we have a project in which all assumptions turn out to be true and all the workaround options work. If a couple of assumptions go wrong, the team is unprepared to deal with them. They often struggle to deliver the project within pre-determined targets.

In the Information Era, where projects are of an experimental or iterative nature, many assumptions are made and many of them have a high probability of manifestation. Being prepared for this is a key factor for sustaining the project, and going towards achieving the objectives of the project. Spiral staircase project management prepares for assumptions that could go wrong and provides shock absorbers for such cases.

Being prepared for unplanned tasks is critical for completing a project successfully. Very often, in today's world, we end up with several aspects of that were not accounted for at the planning stage. They call for additional budget, scope or resources. Many times, these additional steps are essential in order to complete the project or to ensure its stated quality. The project team will thus need to initiate change control process and claim additional administrative justifications.

This, in turn, dilutes the focus of the execution team from the project. As a result, this adds to the complexities of an already complicated project. Often, projects are frozen for additional funding approval. While restarting them, multiple aspects have to be reworked on—which means the need for more efforts when compared to seamlessly executing the project. In addition to these expenses, gaining momentum will also become a challenge, as the rhythm of the progress has been disrupted. As a result, scope creep, amendments and course corrections lead to the divergence of the team's focus. Hence, a framework that offers flexibility and, at the same time, aligns with the deliverable is needed to account for such eventualities.

Principle 4: Effort and effect are not directly proportional in projects

Many of the steps in a project are iterative—so, there is no assurance that every time effort is made to accomplish a task, it will result in the project's progress. Often, tasks have to be performed with multiple iterations in order to advance to the next stage. Hence, measuring the effort as a criterion for the project's progress misleads the KPI that are used for determining the progress of the project. Measurement of the effect or the result is to be considered for determining the true progress of the project. When there are additional iterations that go beyond the initial estimate, the project's contingency funds and resources are to be released in order to accomplish the objectives. This does not mean that unlimited surplus funds and resources should be deployed in a project. Hence, there is a need for a framework that, from time to time, recalibrates the viability of the projects to identify successful ones, in the direction of reinforcing them with needed funding, and prunes out unsuccessful ones without additional spending. While SSPM recognizes the need for flexibility in resourcing for a project due to its iterative nature, it enables detection of unviable projects at an early stage and termination or recalibration of the same at regular intervals. This enables effective deployment of limited resources.

Principe 5: Culture of engagement is a key enabler in projects

Unlike brick-and-mortar projects, a cognitive project is executed by the human mind. Hence, beyond the business boundaries, a project needs to have a sense of belongingness from its stakeholders and, more importantly, from its knowledge workforce. Hence, the purpose of the project becomes a compelling vision for the project team. At the time of creating a vision for the project, the entire team needs to be involved in the process for the sake of understanding and to be a part of it. The planning process can start by involving all stakeholders, who are equally important in delivering a project. The planning process needs to be inclusive for each of the work streams that are going to execute every segment of the project—this will help convert the purpose of the project into a shared vision for each work stream. The teams need to realize the importance of their work and their individual contribution to the overall product; they need to be passionate about what they do. Rather than command and control, the engagement of the stakeholder, sense of ownership and volunteerism makes a difference in today's project.

Principle 6: Projects get influenced by the external environment

In today's projects, there is often need to redefine the entire project during execution, due to external factors. It is now an inherent part of a project ecosystem to recalibrate a product when a similar product is launched in the market space. Hence, if a project team holds on to the original scope and pushes the team towards completion, it assumes that the project is completely insulated from the external environment. The speeds at which new products are adopted in the market space and, on the other hand, old products become obsolete, are increasing every year. Hence, a project needs to be able to adapt to these changes and recalibrate its own assumptions, targets and scope from time to time to ensure its product remains relevant in the marketplace.

Customer behaviors change, devices change faster and technology becomes obsolete rapidly, as newer products are introduced into the world. We are in a world where inventions and innovations grow at an exponential rate—reports suggest that the number of inventions in last two decades is much higher than that of the entire human race till date. Hence, in today's scenario, it is seldom easy to stick to the original scope of a project—flexibility is required to adapt to the rapidly progressing technology and external factors to thrive and succeed.

So far, projects have been executed with an inside-out view. However, the twenty-first-century project also calls for an outside-in view in order to be sucessful.

Principle 7: Projects are like a relay race, not a marathon

The execution of a project has evolved to become a complicated, interdependent endeavor wherein multiple expert groups are engaged at every step of the project lifecycle. The modern workforce has developed into a specialized vertical, such as master builders or the 'one person does all' no more exists. Hence, the one who develops a product does not test it, and the one who tests the product does not release it. There are specialized verticals that have the required expertise to carry out the individual segments of a project. Complex cognitive projects encompass multiple roles, such as innovators, researchers, manufacturers, regulators, technology providers, service providers and quality units. These groups are interdependent and knowledge transfer between them is a vital aspect of a typical project. The risk profile, complexity and pace of these individual segments differ, and cannot be treated the same way. Hence, upfront planning of the whole project, assuming the same modus operandi for the entire project, results in a significant challenge. To preempt this, the planning process needs to engage these domains at appropriate stages. Deterministic models do not address this problem as the baselining is done upfront, and the entire team is bound by those targets until the end of the project—as in a marathon race. In reality, today's project is more like a relay race, where multiple teams participate in the race. Even in an athletic relay race, as stated by Jon Drummond (the 2012 Olympics relay coach for the United States), there are specialists for each of the legs. The first leg requires the most explosive runner; the second, a good long-distance runner; the third, a turn specialist; finally, the fourth, the fastest of the four. The speed of all four runners as individual athletes as well as teamwork at exchange zones while passing on the baton determines their success. As the project progresses, the baton is passed on to various work streams one after another, and there is a need for focus on every section of the project in order to increase the speed of work and meet the intended purpose. The speed of the overall project is determined by the speed of the individual steps of a project. As in a relay race, it is often the current step that determines the speed—not the one that was completed or the one that is coming up. Often, all the accumulated delays are passed on downstream and there is an unreasonably short time limit for the latter-stage work streams to deliver. There is a 'near death experience' at the delivery point of every project for the project team—particularly for the work streams at the end of the project need, to race against the time to meet the project deadline. This team is often required to deploy extraordinary effort to balance between time and quality. This is also a reason why SSPM considers improvement in local optima in order to improve global optima. Like a relay race, every segment has the same commitment and pressure to deliver and individually—they are to be focused on successful execution of their section in order to deliver a project as a whole.

Planning a project as a marathon results in the integration of its stakeholders for the entire width and depth of the project. As a result, there is a tendency to keep everyone involved in the status updates, decisions and resolution of issues. The problem in today's projects is not lack of communication, but overwhelming communication from every corner. Thanks to the Information Age, people get hundreds of e-mails every day, which are related to the entire project. In reality, only a fraction of those would be relevant for their part of the work, and which require a direct response. As in a marathon, people are expected to keep everyone involved in the proceedings. People are busy responding to e-mails, and the remaining time is used for productive work; not reading e-mails is considered an indicator of noninvolvement. This does not allow them to focus on their core work.

To summarize, a cognitive project is a creative endeavor that converts ideas into useful products, services or results. The goal of a project is the purpose it needs to achieve, and all the steps are imperatives that could help in attaining this. Spiral Staircase Project Management values the purpose of a project more than anything else. Progressively elaborate projects are to be progressively planned. Being prepared for something that was not foreseen is required for achieving the purpose of the project. There is always the possibility of undertaking course corrections if a project is not aligned with objectives or needed to get up to speed with the technology and to be relevant in the market space. Hence, there is a need for flexibility in budget and time estimates. Detailed planning of the immediate activities that are known is evaluated, rather than the upfront estimates in the beginning. Spiral Staircase Project Management counts the execution team's ability to deliver the project as it is progressively elaborated. It accounts for scope change where needed, as long as the project is intended to achieve the purpose. It enables fast and nimble behavior than being rigid and inflexible in order to achieve the purpose of the project. This model values flexibility in project execution as long as project is aligned with the actual purpose it is intended to deliver.

> The seven foundation principles behind the framework:
>
> Principle 1: Progressively elaborated projects are progressively planned.
>
> Principle 2: The purpose of the project is the most important goal.
>
> Principle 3: Assumptions can go wrong.
>
> Principle 4: Effort and effect are not directly proportional in cognitive projects.
>
> Principe 5: Culture of engagement is a key enabler in cognitive projects.
>
> Principle 6: Projects get influenced by the external environment
>
> Principle 7: Projects are like a relay race, not a marathon.

Spiral Staircase Project Management Framework

True north of projects and SSPM framework

The purpose of the project is its true north—it is not completing the project on time, and within cost and scope, it is attaining the very purpose that the project is intended to create. At the same time, a project cannot be a bottomless pit that consumes infinite time and unlimited resources in order to attain the purpose. This is especially true in cognitive projects, there is a tendency to keep on fine-tuning the product, as there is always scope for improvement. It is said creative works are never finished, only released—hence, it is important to define the finish line to makes business sense. This raises the need for a framework that enables a purpose-centric approach while having checks and balances to ensure financial viability and business sense. Due to the cognitive nature of the projects, the framework needs to reinforce the interdependency between the work streams to enable practices and behaviors that mutually support each other in the journey towards the true north.

The following is SSPM's five-step process for managing a cognitive project:

1. Project Initiation: Identify a Purpose of the Project Endeavor (POPE)
2. Initial planning and organizing: Create a master plan of the project

3. **Execution and control:** The large project is divided into multiple, rapid-mini-projects called 'fleets.' Every fleet is executed by following four steps—focus, plan, process and move-on

4. **Platform review:** Project health-check at every platform, which enables a go/no-go decision

5. **Project closeout**

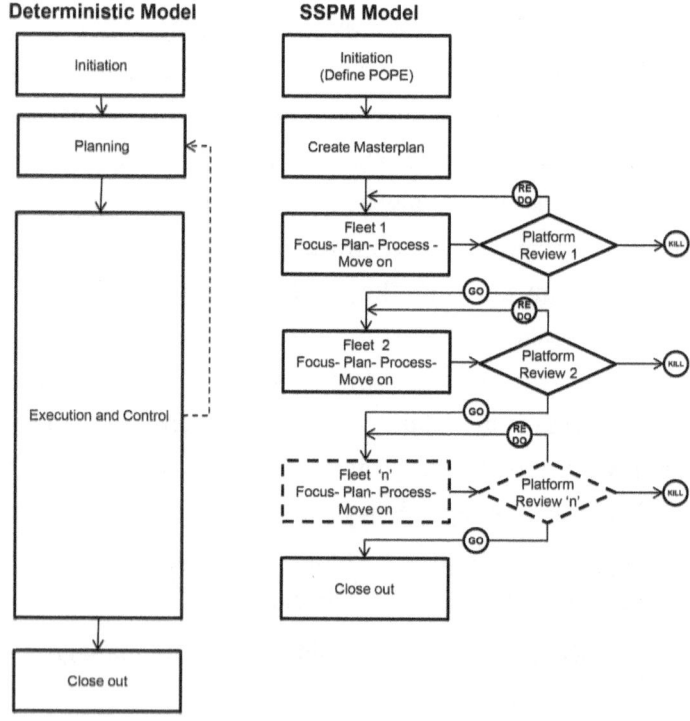

Fig 9: Comparison of deterministic and SSPM model for project flow

Some of these elements depicted in this five step processes exist as bespoke systems or subsystems in many corporate environments and R&D laboratories. The idea here is to take all these practices and create a coherent, mutually reinforcing holistic framework that fosters the purpose-centric design of project management. The ultimate value is to be delivered as objectives, while the 'nominal timeline' acts as a guiding pole.

At the outset, it may seem as if one is getting into a project without a complete plan. It is not about being unplanned but being prepared for unplanned events that need to be completed in order to accomplish the purpose that the project is intended to create. Let us look at every stage of the project in order to deliver the purpose through SSPM.

> *Five core processes of Spiral Staircase Project Management for managing a cognitive project:*
>
> *1. Project Initiation:* Define a Purpose of the Project Endeavor (POPE).
>
> *2. Initial planning and organizing:* Create a master plan of the project.
>
> *3. Execution and control:* The large project is divided into multiple, rapid-mini-projects called 'fleets.'
>
> *4. Platform review:* Project health-check at every platform, which enables a go/no-go decision.
>
> *5. Project closeout.*

The Five Core Processes of SSPM

Core Process 1: Project initiation—define the purpose of the project endeavor

> *All things are created twice; first mentally; then physically. The key to creativity is, to begin with the end in mind, with a vision and a blueprint of the desired result.*
>
> Stephen Covey (Covey S. R., 2004)

The purpose is something that the customer wants from the products, services or results that a project aims to deliver. As Harvard professor Theodore Levitt says, "People don't want to buy a quarter-inch drill, they want a quarter-inch hole!" (Martin, 2009) People buy products and services to fulfill a 'job to be done' or to achieve a goal. Similarly, every project is also triggered by an ultimate purpose or value addition that is to be delivered to the customer. Accomplishing this purpose on time, with the assurance of high quality, achieved within scope and cost are to be considered as a whole to determine if the project is successful or not. We call this the 'whole project paradigm.' Merely completing the project within time, cost and scope may not be a precise way of defining the success of a project as this does not mean that the whole project was delivered. The purpose becomes the nucleus of the project, and determines the project's success or failure. Hence, establishing the core purpose clearly and demarcating it from additional benefits is critical. The core purpose can be delivered by undertaking various efforts. It is important to understand that the efforts themselves are not projects—hence, identifying efforts and purpose and not mixing them up becomes equally important. The purpose of a project is to be identified without any bias, as this is the single most important factor in a project. One of the best ways to determine the purpose is to get the customer to define the core value that needs to be delivered through the project. This might be a new product or an answer to a question, a solution to a problem, a solution to an unmet need, or proving or disproving of a hypothesis. Understanding what the customer wants through the project is vital. It is not an easy task to define this for every project, particularly in novel product development process, as there is no precedence. It is often easy to misunderstand the attributes of the project as the purpose. If a customer is not able to define the value, and comes up with an attribute to describe what she wanted, there are time-tested methodologies such as market research and new-age techniques such as Value Proposition Canvas (Yves Pigneur, 2015) that can be used to define the project's core purpose. The purpose becomes the nucleus around which all of the project's activities are built. For simplicity, we have listed four major kinds of the main project attributes—project, process, product and business. All of these are important attributes, but they would not be needed if the purpose is not delivered.

A purposeless project is like sailing a ship without knowing the destination—it is better not to begin the journey without defining the destination upfront.

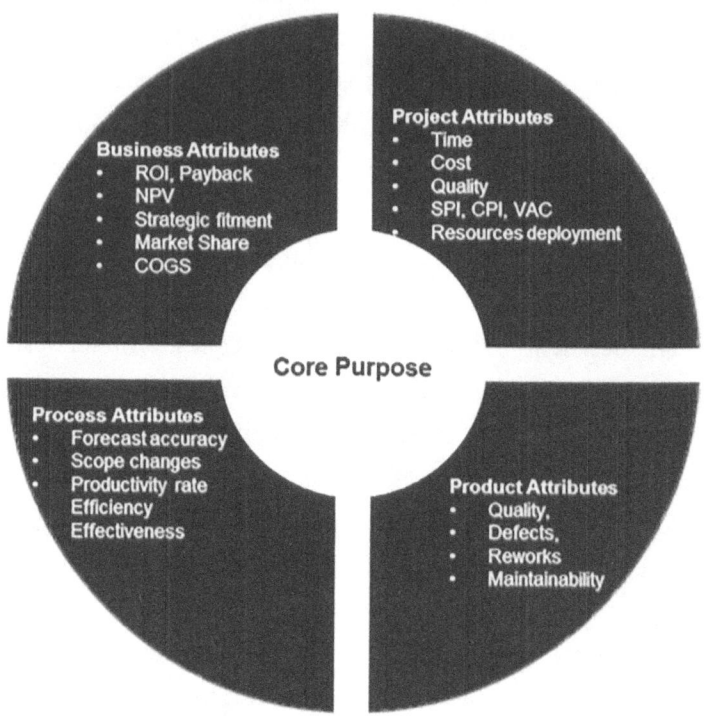

Fig 10: Purpose-centric value proposition of projects

While aligning with the purpose of the project, there is a need to be cognizant of what the customer's needs and wants. According to urban legends, NASA spent a significant amount of money and effort on a project to develop a pen that works in space, but the Russian astronauts solved the problem by using pencils. Irrespective of whether this story is true or not, it gives us a profound message on understanding the core purpose before getting into the wants or 'nice to have' features. Most complex problems have simple solutions, but finding that solution is not so simple. The first step in solving any problem is to understand the problem itself. Methodical analysis of the purpose would lead to the true value delivery of the project.

Align on the purpose with the customer

If less attention were paid to defining the purpose of the project at the initial stage, it would lead to a significant course correction and end up with scope creep. Some of the primary reasons for the new product failure in the market space are fixing a problem that does not exist or creating value that is not needed by the customer. When the purpose of the project needs to be defined upfront, it is often indeed better defined by the customer or end-user rather than by the project managers—this is a critical aspect of the SSPM framework. Also, there is no proxy for a customer or his role in any project management practice. Hence, customer-facing teams may have to support them in defining this at the time of securing the project, and align with them on how it is going to be achieved. Time, cost and scope can be worked out well if the project's purpose is crystal clear. If there needs to be any course correction, the same can be referred to as well. Creating a compelling vision is an essential first step to any creative process, and it is the same for projects as well. Hence, the purpose needs to be defined vividly. The intent is not to create additional documentation—one could just stick to the project charter. This is about value creation that is to be provided to the customer or client. A loosely defined purpose becomes an inherent source of chaos, which results in people pulling in different directions in accordance with their own interpretation. A good charter covers all the aspects of 'what, why, who, when and how' of a project. One can pressure-test their own charter to see if that has all elements of the compass, clock and destination included in the charter (illustrated in picture 8).

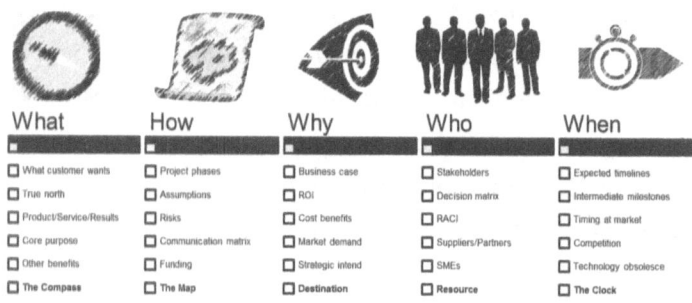

Fig 11: Essential components of a project charter.

The difference in approach in the SSPM framework is to define the 'Purpose Of the Project Endeavor' or POPE, which is the core objective of the project. The well-known 'tree swing' analogy depicts how the customer's requirement is viewed differently by several stakeholders of the project (Høgh, 1993).

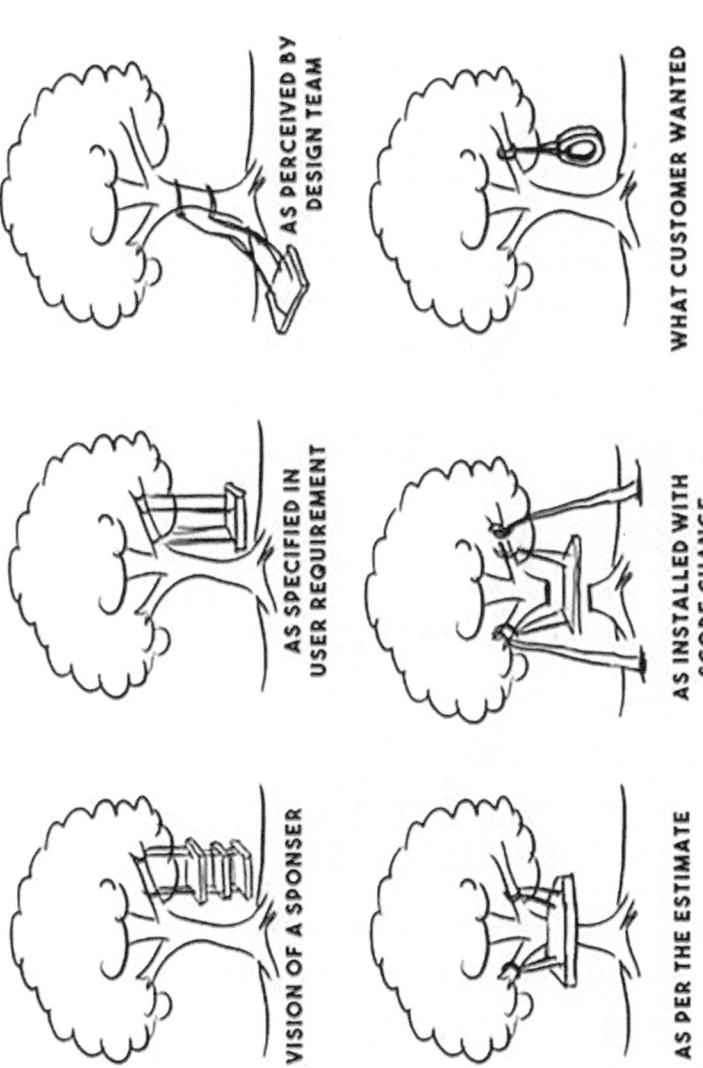

Fig 12: Tree Swing analogy on interpretation of purpose of the project

Tree Swing analogy on interpretation of a project's purpose (Uncertainty surrounds the origins of the tree swing cartoon—the same was adapted with acknowledgment to the source of this illustration.)

The misinterpretation occurs when a project's attributes are taken into account rather than the core purpose. Hence, the more accurately the POPE is defined, the better it is, as all assumptions, risk and mitigation options would refer to this true north. This would be used by the team as a reference point, and they can make course corrections from time to time, if needed.

The POPE could be anything, depending on the type of project and the industry it is applied to. Here are some examples:

- To solve a problem
- To add value
- To alienate pain or add gain
- A question that needs to be answered
- To meet unmet needs of a customer
- To create new needs or markets
- To create a new technology or product
- For a successful startup
- To create capacity or to build infrastructure
- A hypothesis to be proved or disproved

- ➢ For incremental innovation
- ➢ To create a next-generation version of an existing product

Once the charter is finalized, the next step is to create a master plan for the project.

Summary: Project Initiation

Objective	*To define the POPE.*
How to do	*Get to the core of POPE, not attributes of the project and define clearly on the objective.*
Why	*The purpose is the true north of the project—all other attributes are woven around it.*
	A project is successful only when the purpose is delivered, and the same is efficient when it is delivered within time, cost and scope.
	Have the purpose as a core theme of the project to guide the project team while making course corrections and taking decisions.
	To make the project more customer-centric and to focus on delivery.
Deliverables	*Project charter with POPE statement with clear core purpose.*
	Project charter also refers to additional benefits from the project's endeavor.
Documentation	*Project charter: Scope document with POPE.*
Useful Resource	*Refer to the tree swing picture while working out POPE.*

Core Process 2: Initial planning—create a master plan

In the first step, the POPE is identified for a project. The next step is to build a master plan that is designed to deliver the POPE. A master plan is a high-level, directionally correct plan that is to be carried out in order to achieve the project's objectives. Every project has a core flow—the set of sequential segments that are to be performed one after another, towards the final objectives. Defining the core flow is the first step in preparing a project master plan. A master plan is an approximately right schedule where the accuracy of estimates is not the objective—it is a reflection of this core flow, and its progress represents the overall progress of the project. Once the POPE and core flow are worked out, they are divided into several logical segments. We call them 'fleets,' and, in a spiral staircase, every fleet lands on an intermediate platform. Every project platform acts as a transition point where batons are exchanged at these points as in the case of a relay race. Activities to be performed between one platform and another are comprised of several steps. Detailing out this is synonymous to work breakdown structure (WBS) in traditional methodology. These fleets deliver intermittent objectives, which have to be accomplished one after another in order to deliver the POPE. Time, cost and intermediate milestones are to be defined at every stage. The following criteria can be used to work out the platforms:

a. Where the project can be logically divided into segments: *An example is of analysis, development, test and release in a typical software development project.*

b. Where a significant delivery can happen—*such as the development of proof of concept.*

c. Where there is a transition from one work stream to another, *such as research team to production team.*

d. Where there is a transfer of knowledge from one individual or work stream to another, *such as outsourcing part of the project to an external vendor/ partner.*

The number of fleets in a project solely depends on the nature of the project, rigor of execution and quality of decision-making needed. The POPE becomes the core theme, and the flow of the project towards achieving this purpose is represented in the master plan. The fleets and intermediate deliveries are to be chosen in such a way that they represent the overall health of the project. Hence, the focus should be on the flow of the project rather than time—using the compass rather than clock to detail the steps of the project's progress.

Traditionally, at the planning stage, the target is to have an accurate schedule by working out a detailed set of deliverables. There are also numerous assumptions, risks and workaround strategies attached to the plan. However, the more granular the plan, the more inaccurate it will be. This is particularly true when the planning is made in the early stages of the project, with very low visibility of the next steps, and leads to inflexibility in the system.

The steps are not detailed in a granular manner at this stage, except for the first fleet. As the project is progressively elaborated, one may not know the intricacies concealed in further steps, and the accuracy of detailing of each fleet would be better achieved after completing the previous one. Hence, the SSPM master plan can only be a gross plan of the project, which will help in predicting upfront requirements approximately and not accurately. The nominal timeline required to cross every platform, and the resources required are also worked out at this stage. Hence, a master plan gives a good insight into the time, cost and resources needed to complete a project and deliver its core purpose. This is to facilitate a feasibility check and lining up of resources. However, as the individual steps are not detailed, they are only considered as high-level estimates, and the client needs to be aware of the potential variation in time, cost and assumed scope. The variability of these parameters will depend on the degree of uncertainty in the project. It is also vital to plan for bench strength while resource planning, which will enable flexibility from a resource perspective. The size of the bench strength is determined by the degree of complexity of the project.

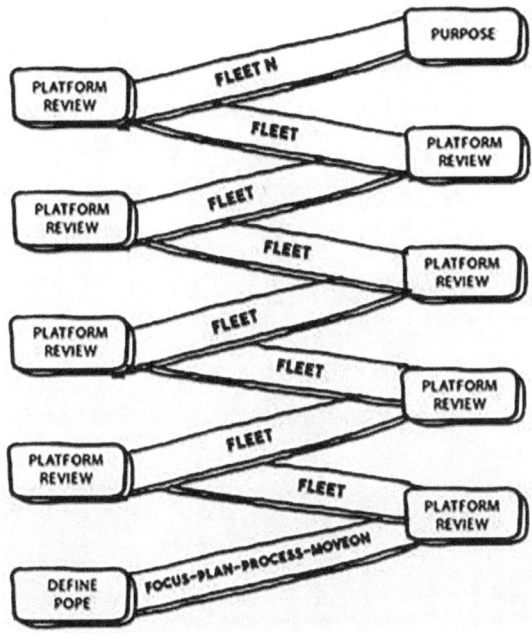

Fig 13: Flowchart of Spiral Staircase Project Management

While aligning with the purpose of the project at every segment of the project, a project charter also has clearly laid out criteria for go/no-go decisions. For example, the purpose may be to develop a product that has a definite drop-dead date for it to be successful. Often, these products have the exclusive marketing rights or tax incentives only if it is delivered on such a date. In such case, the date becomes the true north. If another product is launched first or is missing the date of a tax incentive, the feasibility of the product undergoes a major revision. Such aspects need to be defined upfront as 'go or kill' criteria.

Once the project is divided into several fleets, each fleet needs to be modeled in accordance with a simple input-process-output methodology. Inputs are all that are required for the fleet to be accomplished successfully; processes are the series of events and methodologies to be undertaken in order to convert all the inputs into desired output. Outputs are the intermediate delivery or objectives of the segment, which that are to be delivered. By achieving the outputs of each segments one after another, the project progresses towards delivering the ultimate purpose of the project.

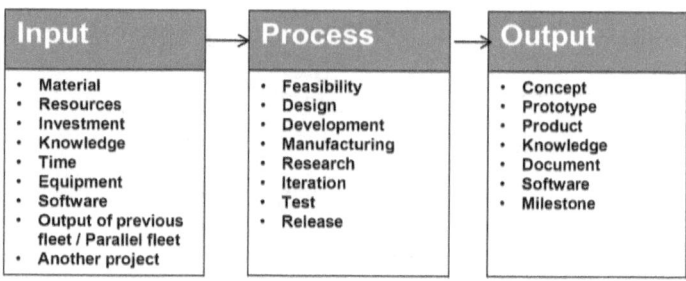

Fig 14: Input-process-output model of project fleets

Input planning: Every fleet requires the materials, men, methods and machines to be lined up in order to successfully finish the segment. Some of the inputs for fleets may be the output from the earlier fleet. While working out these requirements, open items, risks and assumptions are also worked out for every fleet. The unknown factors can be explored to the best extent possible, but many of them would be revealed only as the project progresses. Hence, one has to be aware of this and make appropriate provisions in the budget and/or contingency reserve while working out a master plan.

The objective of this planning is not to be 'accurately wrong' but to be 'approximately right' in estimating the initial time, cost, effort and scope required to deliver the project successfully. Hence, granular details are worked out only for the first few steps, which have clear visibility. No time is wasted in trying to accurately determine estimates of further steps that do not have visibility. Fleet-wise detailed planning and aligning with overall objectives is to be done one after another, after successfully crossing respective penultimate platforms.

When one reaches the top of the staircase—(i.e.) deliver the objectives—he/she can take stock of all the learning and document them.

Let us recap the steps involved in planning.

    a. Work out major fleets and platforms that the project needs to accomplished in order to deliver the purpose to the customer.

    b. Work out an input-process-output model for each fleet.

    c. Work out requirements, assign risks, workaround options and assumptions, and provide for unknown factors in every fleet. This will help develop a high-level estimate of cost, time and resources required. For instance, material to be procured to start the next fleet needs to be worked out and initiated well in advance, in line with the timeline of the next fleet.

    d. Work out a nominal cost, time and resource plan for each fleet.

e. Make a detailed plan of the first immediate fleet, which is at the beginning of the project. Here, the activities can be worked out more accurately until the next platform is visible. This process should be repeated for every fleet.

Assumptions are to be validated for every fleet. Various external factors are to be checked at every step, including regulation changes, technology upgrades, competitors' launches and changes in customer behavior.

Planning is not limited to project schedule development. Depending on the project management maturity of every organization, all the other best practices like communication management, procurement management also needs to be worked out. A detailed schedule can be prepared for the first fleet. When finishing the first one, the second fleet is visible—hence, assemble the project team and chart out a more detailed plan for the second fleet. Do the same for subsequent fleets and continue this iteration until the project's objective is delivered.

Communicate the vision: Once the master plan is created, it has to be communicated to the team. One of the best ways of communicating it is to make the master planning session an inclusive process, by including doers or their representatives. When they become a part of the process, they understand the intricacies of the project and appreciate the POPE that has to be delivered. This is the best way by which the culture of engagement can be encouraged while introducing a project in an organization. The POPE becomes the theme, and the master plan is a map to help achieve the POPE. This can be modeled in different ways, in line with the nature of the business and the company's culture, but the essence is to make it a shared vision for the team. This is vital for an Information-era project, as it encourages the passionate execution of every fleet.

Splitting the project into major fleets also helps in dealing with some of the outsourced segments efficiently. In today's environment, many projects or sub-steps are being outsourced to expert groups internally and externally. Splitting the larger project into mini projects also enables better control over such aspects.

The architecture of SSPM:

In the SSPM architecture, the highest level of the entity is the master plan, which is equivalent to the entire staircase as seen from a distance. A master plan provides a gross schedule, and all the risks and assumptions needed for adequate planning and organizing at the initial stage of the project. One needs to be aware that there will be deviations from the master plan's estimates. These differences will be determined by the level of intrinsic variability and the complexity of the project. Sponsors need to be aware of this, and be ready to deploy additional resources if required.

The second level of the schedule is the fleet, where the master plan is divided into several segments. Every fleet has activities called 'steps,' which are worked out as watertight schedules. These are more granular plans with highly accurate estimates. Just like a staircase that has platforms in-between floors, the SSPM schedule has platforms in between fleets. These platforms play a vital role in ensuring that the project is progressing in line with the core purpose of the project.

A project is not necessarily a linear endeavor which has a single path of execution. There are multiple parallel paths which need to be performed in order to deliver the purpose of the project. In such case, the core path is determined based on the one which reflects the progress of the project and the parallel paths are to converge to respective platforms, where the output of the parallel paths are needed in order to proceed with the projects. Same five step process needs to be applied to the parallel paths considering them as mini projects. The branching out and branching in to be done at appropriate platforms.

Summary: Initial planning—create a project master plan

Objective	Work out the overall flow of the project, and define various segments that are to be delivered in order to attain the ultimate purpose of the project.
	Prepare a complete blueprint of the start to end of the project with initial estimates of time, cost and scope.
	Create a directionally correct plan, but accuracy is not the objective of the master plan.
How to do	Divide the projects into several segments or 'fleets' from start to the end.
	Define input-processes-output for every fleet.
	List down fleet-wise assumptions, risks, and mitigation options.
	Detail various intermittent deliverables and prerequisites needed for subsequent fleets.
	Divide the project based on intermittent deliverables, stages and transition of project through various work streams.
	Do not target for accuracy in estimates for the overall project.
Why	Planning for the entire project does not necessarily result in an accurate estimate due to progressive elaboration. Hence, high-level planning is done where major deliveries are to be achieved in order to achieve the purpose of the project.
Deliverables	1. Master plan of the project: Project-level blueprint plan from start to end, indicating the flow of the project.
	2. Definition of fleets, platforms and associated risks, issues and assumptions for every fleet.
	3. Input-process-output for every fleet. Prerequisites are needed for subsequent fleets in order to line up for the platform.

Core Process 3: Project execution

The project execution approach in this methodology is to systematically convert the master plan into accurate, actionable mini-projects, deliver them with increased value and velocity, and align them to the purpose. In the master plan stage, the project is divided into several segments; at the execution stage, it is carried out fleet by fleet. Two fleets are divided by a platform review process. Every fleet has inputs, processes and outputs, and is similar to mini-projects such as development, production, testing and releasing. The output gained at the completion of a fleet becomes the input for the subsequent fleet. While completing every fleet, overall timing and cost need to be recalibrated based on the progress of the current fleet.

There are four steps for execution of each fleet—focus, plan, process and move on.

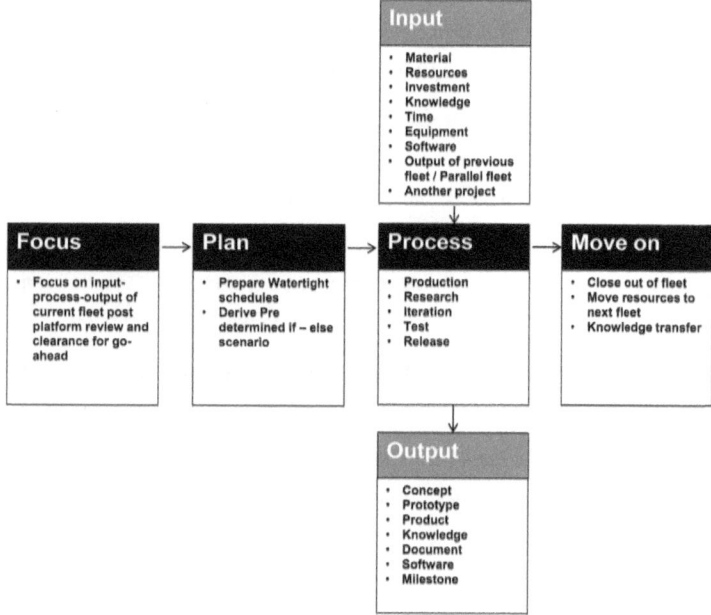

Fig 15: Fleet execution model

'Process' in this illustration is both a noun and a verb. From top to bottom, it is a noun as in the input-process-output model. From left to right, it is a verb as in the case of performing a project.

Focus

This is a process of priming the current individual fleet with all its inputs, assumptions and risks, outlined when the master plan was crafted. As the earlier fleets are completed, and one is near the next fleet, many aspects are revealed, including threats and opportunities—hence, one would be in a better position to explore the same. For example, when one travels in a car, all they see in the light of the headlamps is the next 100 meters. The speed of the entire journey is determined by the way in which each leg of 100 meters is traveled. In the same way, the next fleet that is to be executed will determine the velocity of the project. Hence, the project team focuses on accomplishing the current fleet with rigor and speed. The degree of variability of the uncertain aspects would be relatively less, and can hence be more accurately planned at the beginning of every fleet rather than dealing with the same upfront. While finishing every fleet and getting to the next, the single fleet becomes the focus point of the project team.

Plan

Once the next fleet is taken up for execution and the project team focuses on it, a detailed plan has to be worked out. Today's cognitive workforce is better when it functions as a self-directed team—hence, the planning for the fleet is to be done by the execution team or by a planner, with their consensus. Due to relatively higher visibility on the tasks, assumptions, risks and issues, an accurate plan can be worked out by the team. The level of granularity of this plan depends on the degree of autonomy required for the execution team to deliver the fleet and, at the same time, that is adequate to measure cost and time for that particular fleet.

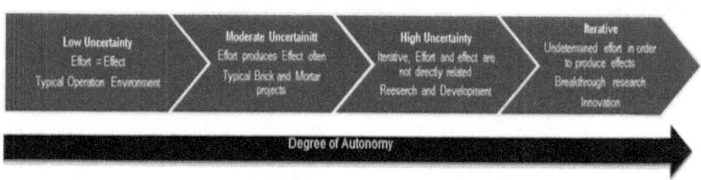

In some of the breakthrough R&D processes, it is possible to undertake multiple iterations to deliver a fleet. However, having gone through the earlier stages, the level of predictability would be relatively larger at this point in time, and an appropriate number of iterations can be considered for fleet planning. Resources and cost estimation would be more accurate in such plan. Hence, the approach here is to develop watertight schedules, which is highly probable for one individual fleet.

Watertight schedules

A 'watertight schedule' is defined as a schedule that is so meticulously planned with highly probable steps, which is impossible to defeat. Preparing this upfront for an entire project is not possible due to various unknowns. However it is possible to prepare for a fleet level under the following circumstances:

    a. *Having completed all penultimate activities of the earlier fleet*

    b. *Successfully passing through a platform review, which provides the 'go ahead' signal to proceed with next steps*

    c. *Steps of the subsequent fleet are progressively elaborated*

    d. *All assumptions can be validated and converted into concrete action items*

    e. *There is no ambiguity in the actions and decisions needed in order to perform activities of next steps*

The characteristics of the steps are to be understood with a view to make a watertight schedule. For simplicity's sake, we can classify the events in a project into two categories—tasks and idle time. Tasks can be broadly classified into two categories—variable and invariable tasks. The duration of variable tasks can be determined by the number of resources deployed in executing the tasks. Sometimes, they can be shortened by deploying additional resources, investment or methods of execution. These are the tasks for which the duration is determined by the number of resources deployed in executing the tasks. If an activity can be done in ten days by one resource, and in five days with two resources, this is a variable task. These tasks can help in shortening or extending a fleet duration, depending on the criticality of the task. Also, this can be modulated to optimize the cost for the tasks. On the other hand, invariable tasks cannot be shortened by deploying additional resources, and require a fixed duration of time to accomplish these tasks.

A simple analogy is traveling from one place to another—it takes ten hours by road, thirty minutes by flight. The duration of the task is determined by the speed needed for this particular activity and relative investment. The cost and time can be balanced to see how fast it needs to move along with the overall fleet speed—hence, it is a variable task. In real-world projects, this is similar to having multiple dedicated teams, hi-tech equipment and automated technology to deliver more precise and faster products versus time-consuming processes.

The duration of invariable tasks cannot be altered by increasing resources or by any other means. A good analogy for this is the incubation time for product testing. If a product needs to be put on hold for six months in stability chambers to see if there is a change in product quality, the time cannot be shortened by splitting it and putting it into more than one stability chamber. Hence, the duration of the non-compressible tasks remains static.

On the other hand, there are idle times that are planned, as well as forced by the nature of the tasks. 'Planned idle time' occurs when the team waits for a key input or material or a predecessor to complete, and 'forced idle time' is by virtue of the project's nature.

A watertight schedule has a series of tasks and idle time one after another, both sequential and parallel, in accordance with the nature of the project fleet. In an optimum schedule, the variable tasks help in playing around with the resources to shorten or lengthen the duration. One cannot do anything about the invariable tasks and idle time, but there are activities that can be planned in parallel so that there is progress even during idle time. If a fleet is to be watertight with respect to cost or time, the same needs to be worked out based on the nature of the fleet. For instance, for products that have high technology obsolescence but a rich margin, time is essential. Hence, the use of additional resources and investment needed to complete the fleet at the earliest should be the approach. If a project is targeted for cost leadership, the watertight schedule can be made in accordance with the cost.

The progress of the project is to be measured in accordance with the advancement of the tasks and idle time consumption. The tasks that result in progress are the ones that lead to the project's progress. These have a direct correlation between effort and effect. Often, some tasks do not result in progress after the first few iterations but will ultimately get completed. The last iteration, which results in the effect, represents the progress. Hence, when multiple iterations are needed in order to produce desired results, it is useful to deploy the available bench strength resources to expedite the progress of the current fleet. This, in effect, results in improvement of the overall project. Measurement of progressive time versus unprogressive time is the best way to measure the performance of the fleet.

If a project, particularly a fleet, has a high degree of uncertainty, it need not be estimated accurately. The rule to be applied is 'approximately right than accurately wrong.' Planning is not for planning's sake, but to guide the project team in order to deliver the fleet faster. Hence, the purpose of the plan is not to stifle execution, but to enable the project's progress.

In many research environments, the effort and effect correlation would vary from one fleet to another. For instance, selection of a prototype for a new product requires multiple iterations and, hence, the accuracy of the fleet is often lesser. It is seldom feasible to estimate accurately how much time and effort will be required for that particular fleet. In the same project, once the prototype is tested successfully and it goes into manufacturing, the uncertainties are fewer. The fleet with fewer uncertainties can generally be provided with granular schedules. Hence, the granularity of plans can be determined based on the type of fleet in a given project.

Process

This is where the rubber meets the road. Once a particular fleet is focused and planned and resources are mobilized, execution begins. Support from the entire organization has to be provided to the execution team because the speed at which every individual step is completed determines the overall timeline. In order to enable velocity, the project team focuses only on one fleet at a time, and resources take on only one task at a given time. It is monotasking that enables speed and not multitasking. It is true that this would depend on the type of the project, and on interconnected activities. However, on the whole, the best way to increase the speed of execution is by monotasking for a work stream or an individual resource, where the changeover time, diversion of focus and distractions to the execution team is minimal.

The velocity of execution is the single most important factor. It is like a relay race where four runners are running the race, but the overall speed is determined by the one who is holding the baton. Hence, the focus is on the one who carries the baton for that moment. The speed of the last player run and the speed of the next player going to run does not count for that moment. Likewise, in an SSPM project, the focus is centered to the fleet that is in progress, and the resources, budget and capacity to be allocated for the current fleet. Also, this avoids the diversion of focus into other activities that may not help the overall health of the project. The idea is not to have any idle time in the project's execution unless it is necessary by virtue of the nature of the activities or the decision to decelerate the velocity for economic reasons. While starting a fleet process, all the prerequisites are lined up upfront, resources are made available, and decisions are taken prior to the fleet start up at platform review—hence, at the time of execution, there is no time to waste. It is purely a well-orchestrated effort to progress the project to the subsequent fleet without idle time. As seen earlier, in turning around the triple constraints, improvement of the velocity of the project execution is the primary benefit of the SSPM project framework. It helps to divide the larger project into several sections, enables focused execution of each resource or work stream through monotasking, and avoids diversion of efforts. It also facilitates the laying out of clear objectives for each section, which is the primary goal for the work stream until the section is completed. Following through with the watertight schedule, a fleet schedule has all four kinds of tasks—variable and invariable tasks, and planned idle time and forced idle time. This enables analysis of the best way of shortening the idle time and improving the progress for every given day of the fleet. In addition to project tasks, meetings and communication are also part of the environment, which sap the time and energy of the project teams. Through the platform review process, all project-level decisions are worked out up front so decisions that require a larger team are taken at this stage. This process enables the work stream to become a self-managed team that requires minimum support from a larger team. The execution team is adequately empowered to take decisions. Hence, the meetings are limited to the aspects pertaining to the particular fleet, and involve the work stream pertaining it. It is critical to provide autonomy for the project team that processes each of the fleets. In the case of any inputs or decisions needed from the larger project team like the sponsors, these decisions to be converted as 'if-else permutations' and authority to take the decisions are to be provided to the project team. This enables the team to focus on execution rather than being caught up in an ambiguous situation at the time of execution. Platform reviews are organized meetings, which help to minimize ad-hoc decisions.

Move On

This is the closeout of the fleet before the team moves on to another fleet. The necessary documentation and knowledge that is to be passed on to the next fleet have to be prepared in order to facilitate a complete, seamless transfer. At the master planning stage, the nominal estimate of time, cost and resources might have been sufficient. Now that this particular fleet is completed, it is a time to recalibrate the project with the actual cost and time taken for completing the project. For instance, if the project has progressed halfway through, the cost and time estimated as part of the master plan and the actual sum of the cost and time taken until this platform was reached will help in assessing whether the project is on track or not.

When Ford introduced the progressive assembly concept for its Model T, with more of a specialist workstation for each of the parts of manufacturing rather than a team of experts for manufacturing a whole car, it revolutionized the industry. In progressive assembly, they focused on local optima, which resulted in increased global optima. Projects have also evolved by harnessing the efficiency of local optima. In several companies, today, project teams consist of various expert groups that specialize in a particular aspect. The progressive assembly practice can be applied to the project domain as well in order to get the maximum from SMEs that handle subsets of the project. This is made possible by ensuring that all that is needed is lined up in advance, so that every fleet can be delivered faster and more efficiently. This is particularly beneficial for programs that consist of many projects done by multiple expert groups for each functional segment of the project. Focusing on improving the efficiency of every section or local optima helps in improving the whole project performance.

When a larger project is divided into several fleets, it gives the benefits of having several mini projects that are easier to manage and quicker to deliver. This offers greater control over intermediate delivery, clear accountability, more accurate schedules, improved focus and increased velocity. Also, intermediate deliveries improve morale by celebrating small victories and milestone achievements for the individual work streams, and enhance the seamless transfer of projects from one segment to another until the finish.

Summary: Project execution

Objective	To focus on and execute on the current tasks of the project with high precision and speed.
	To be able to completely focus on each and every current fleet with maximum possible speed and agility.
How to do	Create watertight schedules for each fleet with required granularity.
	Systematically convert assumptions into actions and forge into the plan.
	Follow the steps of integrated 'Focus, Plan, Process, Move on.'
	Provide additional resources for iterations if applicable.
Why	Local optima result in global optima.
	The speed of the current fleet determines the speed of the whole project.
	Focusing on the fleet that is in progress improves the overall velocity of the project.
	The accuracy of the current fleet, estimated just after completing earlier fleet, is far better than upfront planning.
	Finish with high precision, and no other diversions—monotasking not multitasking.
	After completing the fleet, the project moves on to next fleet through platform review; SMEs to move on to next project in the pipeline and focus on the same.
Deliverables	1. Validated assumptions, mitigation plan finalized for anticipated risks
	2. Watertight schedule for next fleet
	3. Completion of the fleet
	4. Increased velocity of the fleet that is being taken up
	5. Watertight project schedules
	6. Risks and workaround options

Core Process 4: Project controls in SSPM: Platform reviews

The purpose of the project is the primary objective of SSPM, and all other factors are means of achieving this. Platform reviews are aimed at attaining the following at consistent intervals of a project

 a. Completeness assessment of predecessor fleet

 b. Readiness checks for the imminent fleet

 c. Pressure test quality of the progress

 d. Feasibility check of project

When one fleet is completed—and prior to moving onto the next fleet—the platform reviews act as a release checkpoint. Many times, one realizes that a half-done job passed on to the next fleets will create problems later on in the project—hence, the objectives of the platform review is to look at the fleet that was just completed and ensure that all targeted actions were completed in full. Proceeding to further stages of the project without ensuring this would lead to time and effort being spent on sorting out impediments at a later stage, and might even result in disruption of the project. Even small steps that are ignored in the earlier stages of the project become an impediment to progress at later stages. Some common traps include statutory approvals and procurement of components that might be required at a later stage. If there are any pending activities, the team needs to come to a consensus as to whether they should proceed to the next fleet or not.

There are some steps that are critical and should be completed before going to the next fleet, and there are some that are not critical but have to be completed in order to ensure the project's quality. Thus, an action plan needs to be agreed upon by the project team and followed through until completion. Platform reviews cover the following:

1. Check the robustness of the progress so far, to ensure there are no pending actions that could hamper the project's progress in future. This is an inside-out view of the tasks completed so far.

2. Check outside-in aspects—external factors that influence the viability of the project.

3. Play out a handover from one work stream to another if this is applicable for the project.

4. Recalibrate the master plan estimate with actual time and cost until the earlier fleet, and make projections for cost and time for the rest of the project.

5. Plan the next flight with a granular schedule based on progressive elaboration.

6. Business review of the project 'go/no-go' decision for proceeding to the next fleet, if all the above are successful.

7. Quality checks and adjustments or take 'go' or 'kill' decisions.

8. Engage customers or sponsors in the progress and make them a part of decisions.

If a fleet is found to be partially completed or unsuccessful, the options are to repeat the iteration or to proceed to the next fleet with some concrete actions to be completed within a set date. Sometimes, project teams end up with a complete redesign of the fleet or even the project. Many cognitive projects are carried out for the first time, so it is not necessary to have the outcome in the first iteration itself. Hence, it may be repeated in order to achieve the intended deliverables from that fleet. Often, in a research environment, if a project is delayed beyond a specific date, it becomes unviable. Early indicators of such possibilities would be apparent in a platform review. In a portfolio environment, where limited resources are used to deliver a cluster of projects, it does not make sense to continue a project that is not viable. Instead, the resources can be used for a project that is viable—hence, platform reviews play a vital role in terms of recalibrating the project with respect to internal, external and viability aspects and to take a go/kill decision as needed.

Platform reviews are also used to check for external factors—if the viability or business case changes due to the competitive landscape, technological obsolescence or customer behavior. If a project is very sensitive to the external world, and the technology that was developed could be cannibalized by another product or technology, it needs to be recalibrated. As the product life cycle shrinks and technology become obsolete every day, this is a necessary check to ensure that the project is viable.

A go/kill decision may also be taken if the project is not going to deliver the intended value. The earlier the project is killed, the better it is for the organization as the remaining resources and money can be spent on a project that is viable. If failure is inevitable, platform reviews help businesses to fail projects earlier on and without much loss.

Handover process:

In a project, platforms also stand as the handover point from one work stream to another. Platforms reviews enable the collaboration between these two teams, as the transfer of the project happens. The sending team, which has completed the earlier fleet, hands over to the receiving team, which is responsible for executing the next fleet. The sending team can present the progress, lessons learned and challenges faced and pass on complete information and knowledge transfer to the receiving team. The receiving team has the checklist of activities to ensure that this has to be completed entirely, and they will be able to carry out the project from this point onwards. If there are pending tasks, an action plan is agreed upon to complete the same.

Business review

Platform reviews facilitate business review of the project from time to time—not of all stages, but the ones that need to be examined by the leadership. This ensures the leadership's alignment and granting of further resources if needed. While proceeding with a project, there may be many changes in the customer and business environment with respect to strategic, operational and tactical elements—a project is not insulated from these even though it is being executed on that assumption. Traditionally, the project teams are unprepared to take into account of all these changes as this gets checked at the end of the project at the time of product delivery. Sometimes the team realizes that the product is no longer viable for the market. This is a better situation comparing to launching in the market and becoming unsuccessful. This is due to lack of systemic support for consistent calibration of the product viability after the first initial assessment in the entire project lifecycle. In SSPM, this is checked at every fleet. This will lead to go/kill decisions—pruning a project in the early stages is better rather than progressing until the end and realizing that it was not feasible. This way, resources and investment can be diverted to feasible projects earlier as well.

While terminating a project is an extreme measure and may not happen quite often, this review will help in finer adjustments so as to meet the ultimate goal. Pressure-testing the assumptions made at an earlier stage can contribute to work out mitigation options to carry out the project seamlessly.

Every project starts only after the purpose of the project or value to be created is well defined. The purpose to be achieved by traveling through the project staircase—the several flights that the project needs to go through. Once one fleet is passed, the next fleet becomes more visible. Moreover, all prerequisites needed for the next fleet are lined up, including deliverables from the earlier fleet. Take stock of the external and government regulations, and get to know the profile of the competitors and customers if the project is more consumer- or technology-oriented, in order to factor in the refinements in the project plan if required. Sometimes, significant course corrections may be needed. All this depends on the extent to which the project is influenced by the above said factors.

Quality check: Unlike conventional practices, SSPM provides a means of carrying out a quality check at every milestone by design. This helps the project team evaluate the progress thus far and ensure that the deliverables are fully accomplished before moving on to next steps. Also, this validates the assumptions and enables a choice of mitigation options for some of the risks foreseen earlier. At the end of a platform review, the performance report—that covers the project's performance up to this fleet, project metrics, projections and variance report—needs to be handed out to ensure that the current status of the project is communicated to the stakeholders.

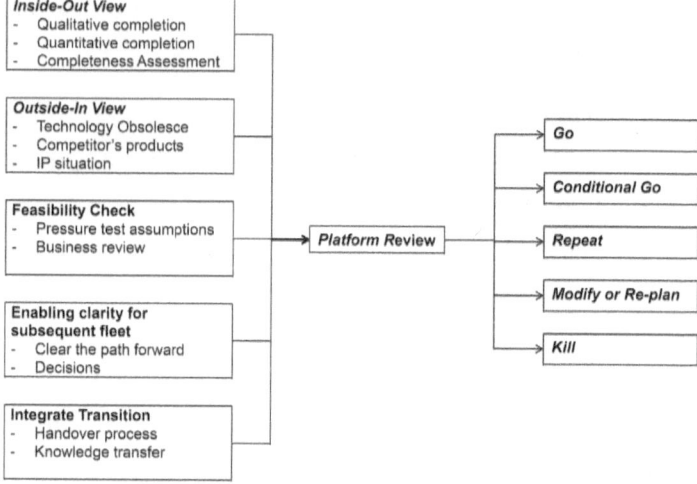

Fig 16: Platform review

Once a platform review is cleared, it means that the fleet after the platform is approved for execution, adequately funded and resources committed. Funding and resources are to be adequately deployed, including additional resources that may be required by virtue of the nature of the fleet. The work stream responsible for the fleet is empowered to execute its portion of the project, take necessary decisions and manage its piece of the project. The work stream operates as an individual profit center of the larger project and becomes responsible for on time, within budget delivery of the fleet.

Summary: Project control—platform review

Objective	*To check the robustness of the progress and preparedness for next fleet.*
	Strengthen the integration between two work streams while transitioning the project to the next fleet.
How to do	*In between two fleets.*
	Completeness assessment of the previous fleet with a checklist.
	Pressure-test to see if the exit criteria have been fulfilled for the project in order to move on next fleet.
	Detail out steps in the next fleet.
	Check if all prerequisites for next fleet are lined up for risk mitigation.
	Pressure-test assumptions made in flow planning stage and make necessary adjustments.
Why	*Manage parts to manage whole.*
	Project's viability will change due to internal and external factors.
	Fosters communication and engagement at regular intervals.
	Enable systematic decision-making.
	Recalibrate project with respect to inside-out and outside-in view
	Identifying and pruning troublesome projects to fail early in order to fail cheap
Deliverables	1. *Quality check of the project progress so far*
	2. *Recalibrate project based on outside-in and inside-out views*
	3. *Go/kill decision*
	4. *Integration of upstream and downstream stakeholders, completeness of handover to downstream stakeholders*
	5. *Check assumption of next fleet*
	6. *Check risk and leverage appropriate mitigation options*
	7. *Overall communication to the organization as on the progress of the project*
	8. *Detailed plan and schedule of subsequent fleet*

Core Process 5: Project closeout—deliver and seek feedback

This involves delivering the project to the customer, step-by-step throughout the project or all together as an end project as per the nature of the product or services, and have a joint analysis to see if the value was delivered. Through the purpose-centric approach and consistent alignment to the project's core purpose at every fleet, the project has a high probability of delivering the intended value. This approach helps the customer to realize the purpose, and the business to deliver the project to the customer without hurdles. All that this framework asks for is to include scope change as a new normal in order to achieve the purpose of fostering the business-client relationship, instead of making it an exception. Usual aspects of required documentation, such as the maintenance manuals, should be undertaken at closeout, as the project is being delivered to the customer. Sign-off from customers and formal closings of contract with internal and external stakeholders are some of the common project management best practices which also need to be carried out here. The extent of these activities and documentation depends on the project management maturity model and culture of the organization.

Closeout plays a larger role in SSPM as the project starts with a directionally correct estimate. This is where the comparison of the estimate of time and cost from the initial master plan takes place. It provides valuable information to ascertain if a company adopted a conservative or aggressive approach in the initial estimate. As the learning curve matures, this would help in appropriately recalibrating the initial estimate closer to reality for further projects. Doing this for several projects, in turn, benefits from the maturity continuum that is developed within the project teams. Through a proper close out process, businesses can develop an internal benchmark for their future projects. Businesses can compare this with external benchmarks to evaluate if they are ahead of the competition and to set the goals for the future. The lessons learned and the surprises handled in any given project are a valuable input for further projects. In Information Era projects, mistakes are acceptable due to the complex nature of the projects. At the same time, repeating the same mistakes shows lack of learning from the past. Hence, the closeout process helps in populating the lessons learned, which can be adapted to other, similar projects as well. This helps in broad-based improvement of the ability to anticipate issues upfront. This helps the project teams to sail towards a maturity continuum for superior performance in future.

To reinforce this process, SSPM also calls for a formal 'knowledge centers' to be established in project organizations, to capture the learning and to keep it as a central repository across projects. While dealing with the cognitive projects, there are several unpredictable events that every project has to encounter. The best way of benefiting from the learning from each project is to apply the same learning to other projects to reduce the degree of uncertainty. Knowledge centers act as a repository of these learning, and can be referred to while planning for a new project or while executing a challenging project. People at the knowledge center would have a fresh perspective on all projects and can actively contribute for master planning, platform review and risk management.

Summary: Project closeout

Objective	To deliver the purpose of the project to the customer or client.
	To conclude that the project has been completed successfully.
	Work out any upkeep or maintenance required for the product or lifecycle maintenance.
	Log the lessons learned so that mistakes are not repeated.
How to do	Check if the POPE has been delivered to customer or stakeholder in full.
	If the purpose is to create a product, if there is a lifecycle element that needs to be taken care, this can be made as a dossier or document and passed on.
	Log all the risks, issues and workaround plans that worked and did not work.
	Establish knowledge centers
Why	Ensure that the product is maintained properly and continues to serve the purpose to the customer.
	The lessons learned help in preempting such mistakes in future.
Deliverables	1. Lessons learned
	2. Product maintenance log

Thus through the five step process, a project worked on in the SSPM framework is executed as well-coordinated mini projects in order to achieve the ultimate purpose. While there are many aspects that are progressively elaborated towards the end of the project, this methodology focusses on executing the immediate fleet or the mini project which is easy to manage and quicker to deliver. Each of these mini projects together constructs the whole project, which aids in achieving the purpose of the project with high focus and velocity.

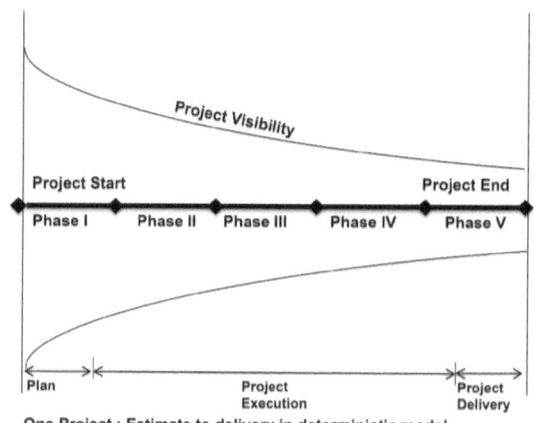

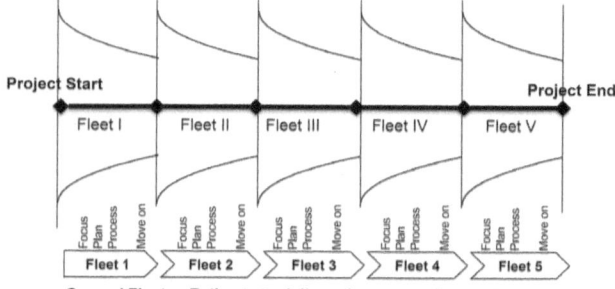

Fig 17: Comparison of the single large project and several mini-projects approach

There is a high chance that the project will have deviations from the cost, time and scope estimates—hence, it is necessary to provide additional provisions in order to achieve the purpose. As this framework is based on approximately right estimates. The project design is flexible enough to deliver products, services and results, so long as the value creation or problem to be solved is defined vividly. This framework accounts for changes in the aspects that the project team does not have control over, such as changes in regulations, competition and technology. The focus needs to be on the flow of the project progress than the progress per se.

It is better to identify and terminate unviable projects early on. An individual or a work stream has only one job to be done at any point of time. They don't have to be burdened with other work that is lined up. Their focus should be on completing the currently assigned task, and then moving on to the next one. Every workstream has its autonomy and pace, designed to get the maximum out of its expertise.

All the obvious decisions, prioritization and 'what-ifs' should be concluded at platform reviews to the best extent possible. Fleets are meant for execution and not decision-making. If there is any ambiguity, it should be dealt with in the platform review process. Experts or SMEs need to focus only on their work—nothing more or less.

Part 4

Program Management:
SSPM for Multi Projects

The multi-project environment has inherent opportunities and challenges. Very often, in such environments, there is a cluster of products that belongs to a portfolio targeted to be developed and delivered in a timely manner. The overall success of the business depends on how many products have been developed and launched in the markets that are successful. In industries such as pharmaceuticals, FMCG, information technology and electronics, bundles of projects are often referred to as portfolios of projects, which are collectively targeted to achieve business results. If launched in a timely manner, these projects often create 'green ocean' market space that results in competitive advantage and early entry opportunities. These are often mutually exclusive yet collectively exhaustive products. New product development with higher margins often becomes a priority to enhance bottom-line growth. Portfolio management focuses on offering a platform of products that are a one-stop shop for customers. It is quite common for companies to offer such products, and keep on improvising them and release multiple versions or upgrades as a part of the product lifecycle. Thus, organizations tide over the product lifecycle and stay ahead of the competition. The differentiating factors are: Who gets to the market first, and how long the product sustains before becoming a commodity.

In such an environment, it is pertinent to have a pool of common resources as project team. Within a project team are subgroups, and every subgroup is assigned to a set of tasks from the project. There are work streams that are responsible for ideation, design, development, scale-up, manufacturing, launch and marketing products. There are common service work streams that deal with a specialized set of services, such as testing, regulatory approvals and quality checks. In such environments, getting the maximum out of the available limited resources is the key to the business's success. Often, projects are timed aggressively as several new products are waiting in the pipeline. In such environments, efficient use of available resources for high value-creating projects is needed to get the maximum from given limited resources.

Failure is a part of the program:

While due diligence is done for selecting winning products for development, real-world experience teaches us that certain products may not see the end of the tunnel. There is bound to be a combination of successes and failures in a new product development environment. In such scenarios, how companies 'responds' to the failure makes the difference, not how it 'reacts.' Businesses often realize that failures also have to be managed a part of the portfolio, along with winning projects. Published statistics shows that a significant portion of the new products does not reach the market. In legacy project management, we have seen businesses deploy more resources and funds in the interest of turning around the failing projects. Some of them do turn around, but many of them do not. In effect, the focus is inadvertently diverted to unviable projects rather than viable projects. Businesses later realize that the amount of effort and time spent on turning around these projects could have been devoted to viable projects—then, they would have benefitted much more. If failure is inevitable, failing fast and failing cheap should be the approach, in order to avoid wastage of efforts of the given limited resource pool. Platform reviews help portfolio organizations to identify signs of such unviable projects early, and handle them systematically in a view to take necessary course corrections or prune out unviable projects. There could be several options to benefit from a project that is evaluated for termination, other than keeping it on the backburner.

1. Sell it off to companies that are interested in such projects. Companies have different risk appetites, overheads and execution mindsets—hence, there could be businesses that are able to undertake a project that is unviable for another. As long as the strategy permits, and is economically viable, these projects could be sold off to other, interested companies, as long as it is mutually beneficial. No project is a bad project.

2. Outsource and keep the project going in case of ambiguity—if it works out, it will be win-win.

3. Assign the project to a turnaround team—often made up of young, enterprising minds. There are several case studies where such teams were able to turn around failed projects (one of the examples is of the 'post-it' from 3M).

Rework, as a result of lacuna at the early stages, blocks the capacity available for another project—and, hence, is to be avoided in a limited resource pool. In lean projects, rework and work on unviable projects are termed as 'MUDA.' If a project is found to be unviable in the later cycle of development, all the resources deployed and investment becomes MUDA. There are options to salvage unviable projects, but the best thing is to pressure-test their viability as a part of identifying the early warning signals. In a limited resource environment, failing early is better than sustaining and failing late. The SSPM model provides an opportunity to determine the early indicators of project viability through platform reviews.

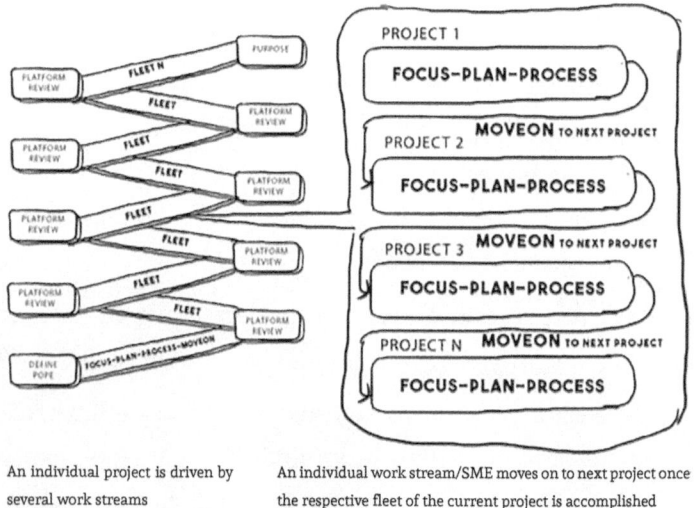

An individual project is driven by several work streams

An individual work stream/SME moves on to next project once the respective fleet of the current project is accomplished

Fig 18: Monotasking of project resources.

While the selection of the products plays a vital role, the speed of product delivery and decisions made at various stages of product development also play a critical role in the overall success. The challenge here is to work on the winning project and improve focus on it. Progressive models such as SSPM are meant for such environments, as platform reviews facilitate identification of problems early on and resolving them before consuming more resources. The specialized workstreams or individual SMEs need to focus on their part of the project, and they have multiple projects to deliver. Through SSPM, they can plan their own activities in a granular manner and be responsible for delivery—this provides a sense of autonomy. The framework enables them to focus, plan, process the current project and move on to the next project. This provides the undiluted focus and power of monotasking. While completing their tasks one after another for multiple projects, they gain mastery over their core area, which helps the portfolio as a whole and improves their pace as their experience builds up. This approach enhances the velocity of the projects, and results in a holistic improvement of the capability of the teams to deliver projects faster and with higher value addition.

The robustness of a project's progress is ensured through platform checks, which enables seamless execution at a later stage. Many times, incomplete or partially completed work becomes an impediment to the project's progress at a later stage—this is avoided in SSPM. Reworking also saps resources in a portfolio environment—it not only needs resources to be deployed unexpectedly, but it also needs the resources to be allocated for the current projects, which hinders the pipeline progress.

The following are four major challenges faced by teams in a multi-project environment:

1. Efficient utilization of available resources for viable projects
2. Getting to the market fast, Improvement in overall velocity of projects to be delivered every year
3. Identifying troublesome projects early and pruning these out from portfolio before additional investments are done
4. Ensuring the robustness of individual projects, so that the lacuna in early stages does not hamper the project's success at later stages

SSPM addresses all the above challenges, and supports the success of portfolios and individual projects. Multi-projects are governed in a similar manner as single projects, with some tweaks to suit the portfolio environment.

Project initiation: Define POPE of the project or portfolio

The purposes of doing all the projects are ascertained—it has to be a single-stop shop for a product platform, or to maximize return on investment (ROI), to deliver an array of new products or to upgrade a technology-intensive product platform. This has to be clearly laid out, and a number of products in the pipeline are to be prioritized. The prioritization could be based on combination of the following criteria:

a. Economic benefits, such as net present value (NPV) and return on investment (ROI)

b. Urgency factor—timing the products that are to be launched in the market

c. Market potential and growth of the product in terms of value and volume

d. Entry barriers

e. Market warfare and competition

f. Early bird advantage—rich margins from new products

g. As a growth engine to sustain a business

All these factors are weighed for each of the products, and priorities are worked out. Generally, the products are prioritized as High, Medium and Low, but the best practice is to give a priority number to each of the products from 1 to 'n' ('n' being the number of products in the portfolio). From this portfolio, the number of products that can be produced with the available resource pool is selected for work. An algorithm has to be worked out for feeding further projects into the active development grid once some of the projects are completed. The final list of products that are selected are put into a 'grid' and projects are assigned to the development team from then on.

Program-level planning and organizing: Create masterplan of individual projects:

Every project is planned with major fleets and platforms. Given that it is a portfolio, most projects have an identical development path. Hence, the project flow and number of platforms remain the same, and evaluation of health and project progress between the products become less complicated. Also, following the same flow will provide a good learning curve for the execution team and provide better visibility to the stakeholders on the status of each project. Templates could be used for planning if most of the projects go through a similar development path. Here is an example of a generic new product development process that could be standard for all products in a typical portfolio:

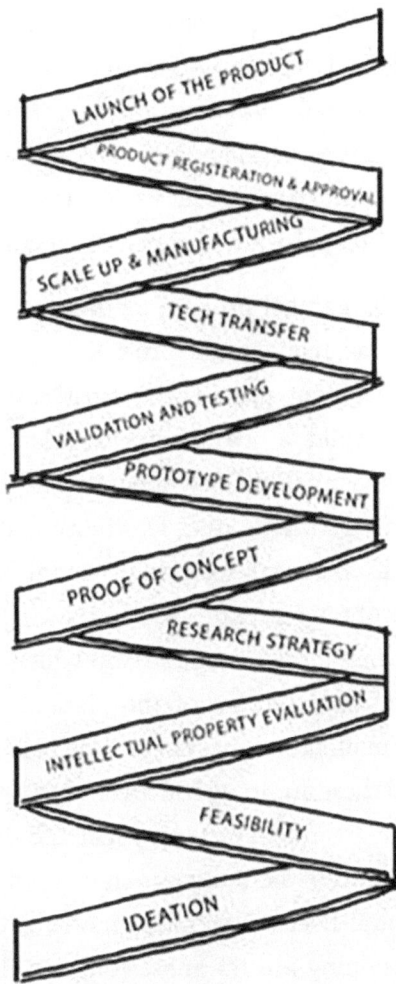

Fig 19: Typical New product development flow

Here, we assume that every project goes through the following flow: Ideation—Feasibility—Clearance on patentability and non-infringement—Research strategy—Proof of concept—Prototype development—Product validation and testing—Tech transfer—Product manufacturing—Product registration and approvals—Launch of the product.

There could be parallel projects or fleets as well which is feeding into the mainstream project. In the case a new product development project, the most common parallel project is to build a manufacturing plant to create a production capacity of the new product. The trigger for this can be as early as the product feasibility and this need to be delivered as an 'input' for product manufacturing fleet. In the course of the entire project, various inputs are going from the product development stream which is needed for designing and construction of the plant. Every platform review of the main project has checks and balances available to ensure that these are going concurrently. The build out the project can be greenfield or brownfield and depend on the size and complexity, the build out staircase need to have a single or several fleets. Design, Engineering, Construction, and Commissioning are the most common fleets of build out project which converging into product manufacturing fleet of the product development project. Parallel projects like this are also to be worked out and integrated into the mainstream project appropriately in order to deliver the POPE of the project successfully.

It is not necessary that all these parts have to have a platform in between. From this project flow, the fleets are to be selected based on the visibility from one stage to the next critical delivery. Other factors used to define fleet are handover from one work stream to another, and major deliveries that need to be checked for ensuring robustness of the project. The following is an example of fleets that are selected for planning and tracking from the larger lifecycle of the product development:

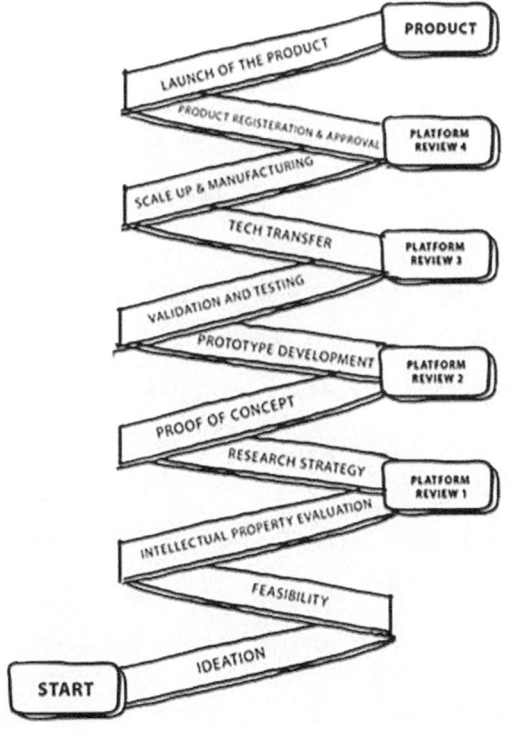

Fig 20: Selection of fleets from typical new product development flow

Reasons for deciding on these major fleets is as below

S. No.	Fleet Definition	Reason for selection
1	Feasibility	Logical end of exploratory study and prior to getting to the actual research
2	Finalize Proof of concept	Major delivery
3	Prototype validation	Major delivery
4	Product scale up and manufacturing	Major delivery
5	Launch	Major delivery and closeout

The basis for selection of fleets is:

a. There is relative visibility from one delivery to another and accurate planning can be made until the next delivery

b. Transition from one work stream of the organization to another

c. Where there is a need for a go/kill decision

d. Critical milestones that represents overall health of the project

e. Deliveries that can be assigned with a timeline and cost estimate to it

f. Major delivery and closeout of the project

The number of fleets will depend on the rigor of execution and quality of decision-making needed for such products. The objective is not to micromanage but to provide leadership and support to the development team depending on the sensitivity of the product being developed. For instance, a product with high technology obsolesce will have a shorter time cycle and also more periodic platform reviews. Baseline timeline and cost targets for each fleet in every project are defined and baselined on a yearly basis, or per the review cycle. In effect, there is a calendar of major platforms to be delivered for all priority products. A sample calendar is as shown below:

Month Target	Platform 1	Platform 2	Platform 3	Platform 4	Platform n (Finish)
Jan	Project A	Project B			Project F
Feb			Project B		
Mar	Project C	Project A		Project B	
Apr	Project D				
May		Project C			Project B
Jun					
Jul	Project E	Project D	Project A		
Aug			Project C	Project A	Project A
Sep	Project F		Project D		
Oct	Project G	Project E		Project C	

Project execution and control: Each current fleet of individual projects is in focus in the program environment. Every individual fleet, upon successful handover from the previous platform review, goes through the focus-plan-process-move on steps. All the prerequisites needed for every current fleet are organized. The platform review ahead of a fleet ensures that all risks, assumptions got checked. Hence, the executor of this fleet not need remain idle or hold the projects for any decision or consensus, as all that is needed is worked out at the platform review level prior to execution. Their motivation is to finish the fleet of the current project at the earliest and move on to the next project. A more accurate and granular plan for this fleet can be prepared as the visibility of the next fleet is greater. As there is no ambiguity, the approach is to focus, plan, process and move on from one fleet to another. The best way of getting this done is to assign one fleet to a subgroup or assign a task to a team member. Once the current fleet or activity is completed, the second one is assigned to the team. This way, undiluted attention is provided to the execution team, and the overall velocity of the program improves. As the process matures reduction in changeover time between fleets and improvement of efficiency due to monotasking is feasible. This translates to managing parts to manage the whole program.

Project control—platform reviews. Platform review helps not only to ensuring the robustness of individual projects' progress, but also to identify and prune unviable projects at an early stage. Thus, it plays a vital role in identifying and eliminating unviable projects at an early stage, which results in efficient use of the available resources.

Developments in external environments are also checked at every platform of a project. Financial viability is also checked. Moreover, ensuring the quality of the progress of all upstream fleets makes it possible to ensure that the projects move without any unfinished works that might hinder project delivery at a later stage. Platform reviews help to pressure-test assumptions, evaluate foreseen risks and select the appropriate mitigation option for the next fleet. Here, too, the prerequisites needed to execute further steps are checked. By managing parts of the projects more efficiently and improving the velocity of the individual fleets, the overall speed of the projects improves results in faster delivery of the portfolio and time to market.

Project closeout: Once all the fleets are completed and the final platform review is passed, the individual projects are properly closed. Lessons learned and any lifecycle management of the product needs to be logged. The objective here is to check that the purpose of project endeavor has been delivered to the customer.

Lessons learned are logged so that similar errors do not recur for a typical project in the portfolio. In a research environment, it is common to learn from trial and error. In a highly cognitive work environment, there needs to be a certain degree of tolerance towards mistakes. This not only enables improved risk appetite, it also results in increased innovation and better creative processes as a whole. This depends on the industry type, and a new mistake could be the next breakthrough invention in the industry. While mistakes are expensive in a new product environment, some mistakes are precious too. Some examples of these are inkjet printers, X-rays and 3M's post-its. The microwave beam was accidentally discovered by Percy Spencer while he was working on energy sources. There are several other examples including, Penicillin as antibiotic, which were invented as byproducts of other major experiments. Hence, by approaching mistakes or failures in cognitive projects differently, businesses could benefit, too.

Profile of Project Leaders in SSPM

While it is an enabling framework that provides flexibility and agility, the SSPM model also requires a new skill set for project managers to manage such projects. Project managers in today's complex, cognitive projects need to come out of the efficiency-centric mindset and become purpose-centric leaders. In essence, project managers are to be transformed into leaders who fosters collaboration. Gaining velocity and maximizing the value with the master plan framework requires clarity of purpose and the ability to bring the team together towards 'true north' of the project. Hence, a project manager has a larger role as a leader of the project, than one who controls the metrics. A project manager needs to champion the entire flow of the project and act as an integrator between work streams. He/she is an evangelist of purpose at every step of the project who possesses the 'big picture' while increasing speed, value and enabling autonomy of the project resources.

A project manager is like the mini-CEO of the project. Having POPE as the vision and the client as one of the important stakeholders of this business, the project manager drives towards creating the business results. As the project teams are focused on the individual fleet, the project manager moves between work streams and propels the project toward the common objective.

When it comes to managing projects, four generic questions have to be addressed:

a. What should the size of the project management team be?
b. Do we need an independent project manager or a team member who can handle project management and execution simultaneously?
c. Is it a part-time or full-time assignment?
d. What should the extent of empowerment for project management be?

The size of the project management team: It is necessary to have a person or a team exclusive of the execution team as part of the project management team. The size of the team depends on the size and intensity of the project. It is a new norm to have geographically diversified project teams—this also determines the number of project managers needed. In the case of multiple project managers, the team lead assumes the chief role and needs to have broad-based visibility of the project.

Independent project manager or execution leader: The two roles require completely different profiles, competencies and focus. An exclusive team member is required, as we need someone to see the project from a different perspective. A common dilemma is whether we should have an independent project management or development leaders as the project managers to lead the project teams. Take, for example, pilots and the operations in the airport. A pilot is well trained and aided with all the automated equipment to fly and land a plane, but air traffic control from a control tower is essential to lead him/her safely. A pilot cannot captain an aircraft and handle air traffic control at the same time. Likewise, in projects, there is a need for an independent project leader to oversee all the aspects in line with pre-determined objectives. Moreover, in SSPM, project management is a full-time job—hence, it is vital to have an independent team leading these efforts.

Full-time or part-time: It is certainly a full-time effort. A project manager can take on multiple projects at the same time but cognitive projects require a full-time project manager.

Empowerment: As indicated earlier, a project manager is the CEO of the project, and he/she is responsible for the success or failure of the project. It is essential for a project manager to have end-to-end visibility and leadership of the entire project, as no one else has this visibility in the SME structure of an organization.

Fostering Change and WIFM

> *First, you know, a new theory is attacked as absurd; then it is admitted to be true, but obvious and insignificant; finally it is seen to be so important that its adversaries claim that they themselves discovered it.*
>
> William James (James, 2008)

Changes in project management methodology, which are in line with the DNA of the project, are essential for any business that wants to not only survive but to thrive in the complex, constantly changing, fiercely competitive and fast-paced world. While the SSPM framework is easy to understand and adapt, it is much more challenging comprehend at a conceptual level. We must recognize that it is not as easy to make a paradigm shift from a concept that has been practiced for ages. While acknowledging that this shift is a challenging one, one needs to overcome execution hurdles for any initiative to be deployed successfully in an organization. At the first instance, the SSPM model may look like getting into the execution of the project without a complete plan, which is unconventional when compared to traditional practices.

Firstly, no change is required if the current project management framework works in an organization, and at least ninety percent of the projects are finished on time, and within budget and scope, this means the existing practice is working well. The change is needed only when the current practices do not produce results. While the deterministic model advocates upfront determination of all targets, SSPM aims to provide flexibility and enables speed by pragmatically dividing the entire project into mini projects. While there is high-level planning at the initial master plan stage, the actual planning is carried out at every fleet as rapid, short-cycle mini projects. While the former provides the ability to line up investment and resources, the latter provides an accurate definition of work and enables the resources to focus on execution.

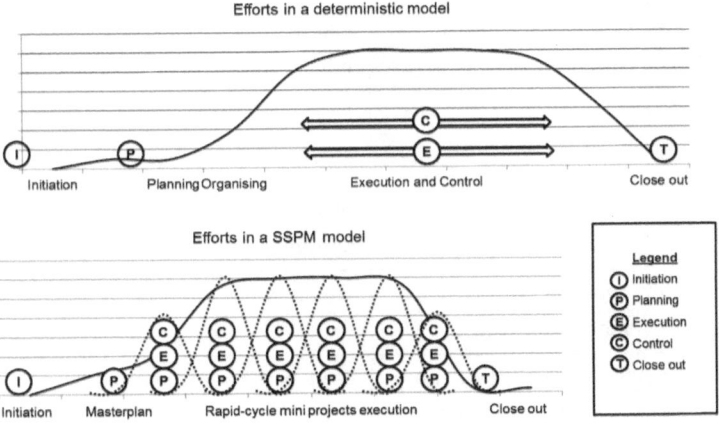

Fig 21: Comparing five core processes of project management.

A comparison of the lifecycle of a deterministic model and SSPM illustrates that the project has a good opportunity to finish early though rigor in execution by converting a long cycle project into several short lifecycle mini projects. In deterministic models, the planning is done upfront and the project team undergoes prolonged execution mode. In SSPM, the same has been done in every fleet, which provides several mini project-cycles within a larger project. This provides better command over the sub-processes of the project. The short lifecycle projects make scope changes and related documentations irrelevant.

Deterministic Model	SSPM
Control cost	Enhance value
Control time	Improve velocity
Control scope	Focus on purpose
Targets accuracy	Targets delivery
Plan upfront and follow the plan until finish	Plan at every fleet and deliver as mini projects
Everything can be determined upfront	Project unfolds and tasks progressively elaborated Many aspects are not known upfront
Everything shall go in accordance to the plan	Things can go wrong
Everything needs to be planned upfront	Be prepared to do unplanned tasks
Make assumptions while planning if things are not clear	Assumptions can go wrong and the project team needs to be prepared for handling the same
A project is like a marathon	Project is like a relay race
Command and control	Adaptable and nimble
Speed of the project is based on speed of the critical path	Speed of the project is based on speed of the current step

Deterministic Model	SSPM
Global optima	Local optima lead to global optima
Aim is to accurately calculate the time cost and define what is in scope and out of scope	Aim is to work out an approximate master plan initially and systematically convert to accurate watertight plan at every stage when project is progressively elaborated
Command and control	Flexible, adaptable approach
Project-centric	Purpose-centric
Unprepared for changes Changes result in scope creep	Change is a part of project lifecycle
Course Correction as a part of deviation	Course correction as a part of the process
Static planning process	Dynamic planning process
Large project life cycle	A project consist of several rapid short-lifecycle mini projects

Some of the profound change management theories and models help in overcoming the hurdles of implementation of spiral staircase project methodology, given that the organization develops consensus to build on the new concept for improvement of the projects and programs. However, changes are intensely personal, and it is vital to gain conviction during deployment, as most of the work in today's world is being done through the knowledge workforce. There are 'what's in it for me' factors to be considered as well while adapting the spiral staircase methodology.

Flexible approach

In the spiral staircase methodology, the total cost, time and scope needed to deliver a project is not accurately calculated or defined upfront, and are rendered flexible, based on initial master plan estimates. At first, it may look like a major hurdle while initiating a project. The reality is that—whether planned or otherwise—scope creep or time extensions or cost escalations result in additional investment. There could also be a compromise in the delivery of the product, services or results to the customer. Spiral Staircase Project Management provides a framework to systematically approach these excursions in a project, and provides a seamless way of accounting for them without impacting the focus of the project. Instead of trying hard to precisely estimate time and cost, SSPM provides flexibility and prepares the team to handle any increases from the initial estimate.

Changes are a part of the process

In traditional approaches, deviations are handled through scope change and time extensions that often damage the relationship between the customer and project companies. With the traditional practices, every project has a 'point of no return,' where the customer has already committed certain costs. Under such circumstances, the situation does not offer an exit option for the customer, and they need to either agree to a scope creep or a compromise in delivery. Spiral staircase methodology prepares them for such deviations, while clear decision points and exit options enable the viability of the project throughout the project lifecycle. Customers or sponsors, in some cases, need to be part of the process while rolling out such programs. In SSPM, the purpose-centric approach puts the customer first and project second.

To benefit from mini projects

Every fleet is like a mini-project in a larger project. The work streams or SMEs that are involved in each of these mini projects have tremendous clarity and have a day-to-day prioritization of tasks. They become responsible for the delivery of their own work stream and celebrate their achievements. This enables autonomy of these work streams and they gain mastery in their field of work. Experience with this methodology helps the organization to look at the areas that need to be reinforced and to balance the entire lifecycle. Mini projects are easy to manage and quick to deliver.

The power of self-managed teams

This framework facilitates the empowerment of the individual work streams that are executing the projects. In a portfolio set up, this leads to several self-managed teams that are responsible for a part of the project. They develop mastery by completing fleets repeatedly one after another. Workstreams participate to a greater extent in planning and target setting of their own activities, and are accountable for delivering the same. The morale of the individual work stream and resources in every fleet will be enhanced by the new approach, and they will feel a sense of accomplishment when each of the fleets is completed. The traditional methodology does not compartmentalize and does not provide absolute clarity about the individual work streams' deliverable, and often results in lacuna being passed on from previous work streams. The SSPM model is designed to avoid the potential turf war between work streams, but reinforces the interdependency between them.

Pre-empt the lacuna in a project

In deterministic models, some of the lacuna gets passed on, unnoticed, to a stage where it hinders the progress of the project in downstream segments. Not noticing this will cause unnecessary delays in the project at a later stage. More importantly, if the product is passed on to the market with this lacuna, this might determine the success or failure of the product or at least have a greater level of influence in customer experience. Through its platform review, SSPM has checks and balances in place to make sure that those aspects are preempted.

Lean communication

There are two levels of communication in this framework—master plan level and fleet level. While the master plan level focuses on all the project level aspects, the fleet level communication is within teams that are executing the mini projects. Fleet level interactions are focused on day-to-day tactical issues, and can be informal to facilitate faster communication and rapid decision-making. The technical decisions that pertain to that fleet are effectively managed at this level. Larger issues that have implications for the project are floated up to the master plan level. Designing the fleet construct such a way that it gets into the master plan level at the platform review is an effective way of doing this. The SSPM model simplifies the communication to a larger extent by having mini projects. While it enables communication across the organization on the overall health of the project through its framework, it also improves the communication within expert groups as focused subgroups. This makes 'copy to all' unnecessary.

Decentralize—empowerment of the execution team

Individual work streams are no longer required to abide by the 'one size fits all' project schedule, made at the start of the project. The plan can be aligned with the individual work streams. The SSPM model decentralizes the project and enables each of the work streams to deliver its best. The necessary budget and resources needed for a fleet are cleared in the platform review. This requires a high level of trust and mutual accountability from the work streams. They operate as individual profit centers in a larger project

Get to market fast

With this new approach, there is no time for scope change and bureaucratic muddle that stifle the progress of the project. Everyone knows their role in the project, and it is performed step-by-step, with absolute focus and clarity. The project successfully passes through the platform reviews one after another and delivers the ultimate purpose or gets reprocessed or pruned if it is not in alignment with the objectives. There is absolute clarity on who needs to do what needs to be done, why it needs to be done, and when it needs to be done. This, in effect, ensures the fastest way to get to the customer in this competitive market. Even a good product, if launched late in the market, may not fetch the full potential of the market. Hence, speed to the market is the objective of the new approach, and this is achievable through its focus, clarity and well-calibrated review process.

Project management is today a management discipline in its own right, and is becoming an increasingly important element of business processes in order to create capacity and Blue Ocean opportunities. Projects become an inherent process in the startup and innovation endeavors. Today's projects depend more on the brainpower of knowledge workforce than horsepower of equipment. The efficiency-centric project management models are more appropriate for Industrial-era projects, where most of the work was performed by machines. Baffled with these models for their knowledge workforce, businesses struggle to deliver cognitive projects every year. In the Information Era, projects are complex and cognitive—a paradigm shift is required to bring best from the knowledge workforce.

- From controlling chaos to unleashing potential
- From rigid deterministic practices to flexible, agile and nimble framework
- From desperation of meeting targets to inspiration of producing surpassing results
- Systematically dividing a large project into several easy to manage mini-projects
- From one person does all or 'master builder' to several subject matter experts to undertake each section of the project

It is evident that surpassing results can be delivered, given that there is an adaptable and flexible framework that enables speed, value and purpose. A purpose-centric culture can enable focus on the project and deliver better results than by controlling timelines, scope and budget. Projects are executed by multiple expert teams, as in the case of a relay race, and performance of all these individual stakeholders' leads to the success of the project. Having a spiral staircase as a metaphor, this framework facilitates simplification of project management practices and unleashes the knowledge workers' potential in order to deliver results surpassing normal standards.

You don't have to see the whole staircase, just take your first step, the rest will be shown to you.

Martin Luther King Junior

Today's projects are unique expeditions, like a relay race in a spiral staircase. A relay race depends on all of its runners to perform the best and likewise a project also relies on the involved teamwork in order to deliver the true purpose of the project. A spiral staircase is a metaphor for not having upfront visibility of all that is needed to deliver the purpose of the project. Given the complexity, visibility and variability, project teams have a challenging but exciting task of reaching consensus on the true north of the projects. Once aligned to the purpose, the SSPM framework enables an increase in velocity, improved value and focus on purpose through its mutually reinforcing practices. There is a shift from command and control to unleashing the knowledge workforce's potential. I am sure this model will help in navigating people-centric and purpose-centric projects.

About the Author

John Robert has over twenty years of experience in projects, engineering, supply chain management and operations. He has significant experience in large-scale infrastructure projects and complex program management of new product development. John completed his post-graduation in business administration in Loyola Institute of Business Administration, and a Bachelor of Technology in Chemical Engineering from the University of Madras.

Currently he is associated with Sun Pharmaceutical Industries Ltd., a global leader in the generic pharmaceutical industry, as Associate Vice President and is responsible for project management of new products development. Earlier, he worked with both infrastructure projects and new product development programs, and has comprehensive experience in brick-and-mortar projects and complex, cognitive projects.

He started his career as a project engineer who designed and constructed manufacturing plants and worked his way through various roles, including consultant, client, end-user, project manager and a leader. This offered him all-round, 360-degree insights on projects. He had the opportunity to envision, institute and lead project management offices for construction projects as well as R&D program management, which provided hands- on practical perspectives of project management. The companies he was associated with had their own level of project management maturity—this helped him to gain on-ground experience, understand challenges observe the way in which projects are planned, performed and managed. John lives in Vadodara, India with his wife, Santhana Mary and daughters Sheron and Thanya.

He seeks opportunities to address some of the unquestioned, conventional management practices. John is now an author with this debut book, and waits to see if you resonating with the same ideas in the area of project management.

He can be contacted though email (johnrobert99@gmail.com) or LinkedIn (https://www.linkedin.com/in/johnrobertmanuel)

Glossary of Terms

CCPM	Critical Chain Project Management
CPM	Critical Path Methodology
FMCG	Fast Moving Consumer Goods
FTR	First Time Right
GANTT	A Gantt chart is a type of bar chart, devised by Henry Gantt in the 1910s, that illustrates a project schedule.
Intrapreneur	A person within a large corporation who takes direct responsibility for turning an idea into a profitable finished product through assertive risk-taking and innovation.
KPI	Key Performance Indicator
MTBF	(mean time between failures) is a measure of how reliable a hardware product or component is.
MUDA	Muda (無駄?) is a Japanese word meaning "futility; uselessness; wastefulness," and is a key concept in the Toyota Production System (TPS) as one of the three types of deviation from optimal allocation of resources (the others being mura and muri)
NPV	Net Present Value
Parkinson's Law	Work expands to the time available
PERT	Program Evaluation Review Technique

PMBOK	Project Management Body of Knowledge
POPE	Purpose of Project Endeavor
POS	Probability of Success
PRINCE2	Projects In Controlled Environments, version 2
R&D	Research and Development
ROI	return on investment
SME	Subject Matter Expert
Student Syndrome	A tendency to procrastinate until the last moment
TAT	Turn Around Times
Watertight schedule	A schedule that is meticulously planned with highly probable steps so as to be impossible to defeat
WBS	Work Breakdown Structure
WIFM	What's in it for me?

Bibliography

Covey, S. R. (2004), *The 7 Habits of Highly Effective People.* Free Press; Revised edition (November 9, 2004).

Covey, S. R. (n.d.). *Leadership: Great Leaders, Great Teams, Great Results.* Franklin Covey.

Dan Ariely, U. G. (2005). *Large Stakes and Big Mistakes.* Federal Reserve Bank of Boston, Working Paper No 05-11.

Høgh, S. (1993). *The tree swing graphic.* http://www.businessballs.com/.

http://www.businessdictionary.com/definition/value.html. (n.d.).

James, W. (2008). *Pragmatism: A New Name for Some Old Ways of Thinking.* Cosimo Inc.

Luft, J., & Ingham, H. (1955). "The Johari window, a graphic model of interpersonal awareness," *Proceedings of the western training laboratory in group development.* Los Angeles: University of California, Los Angeles.

Martin, D. (2009). *Secrets of the marketing masters: what the best marketers do and why it works.* Amacom.

Michael Bloch, S. B. (2012). *Delivering large-scale IT projects on time, on budget, and on value.* Mckinsey Article.

Morris, P. W. (2013). *Reconstructing project management.* Cambridge, MA: John Wiley.

O'BOYLE JR., E. a. (2013). THE BEST AND THE REST: REVISITING THE NORM OF NORMALITY OF INDIVIDUAL PERFORMANCE. *Personnel Psychology.*

Pink, D. H. (2006). *A Whole New Mind: Why Right-Brainers Will Rule the Future.* Riverhead Books; Rep Upd edition (7 March 2006).

Pink, D. H. (2008). *Drive : The Surprising Truth About What Motivates Us.* Riverhead Books.

PMBOK. (n.d.). *Project Management Body of Knowledge.*

Yves Pigneur, G. B. (2015). *Value Proposition Design: How to Create Products and Services Customers Want.* Wiley.

List of Illustrations

Fig 1. Traditional deterministic model project lifecycle and efforts in every phase of the project.. 8

Fig 2. Johari window—applying to unknown unknown aspects of a project 20

Fig 3. Estimate, commitment and delivery in deterministic model 31

Fig 4: *Table: Project ecosystem of various ages* 41

Fig 5: Transforming triple constraints from control paradigm to opportunity paradigm 48

Fig 6: *Linear Staircase Metaphor and Visibility of Steps Ahead* 62

Fig 7: *Spiral Staircase Metaphor and Visibility of Steps Ahead* 63

Fig 8: Visibility of steps in a spiral staircase 65

Fig 9: Comparison of deterministic and SSPM model for project flow....86

Fig 10: Purpose-centric value proposition of projects..90

Fig 11: Essential components of a project charter. 92

Fig 12: Tree Swing analogy on interpretation of purpose of the project 93

Fig 13: Flowchart of Spiral Staircase Project Management............................99

Fig 14: Input-process-output model of project fleets 100

Fig 15: Fleet execution model 106

Fig 16: Platform review 124

Fig 17: Comparison of the single large project and several mini-projects approach 130

Fig 18: Monotasking of project resources. 138

Fig 19: Typical New product development flow 143

Fig 20: Selection of fleets from typical new product development flow..145

Fig 21: Comparing five core processes of project management.................155

www.ingramcontent.com/pod-product-compliance
Lightning Source LLC
Chambersburg PA
CBHW020655220526
45464CB00001B/445